HOW A MAN

OVERCOMES DISAPPOINTMENT AND BURNOUT

LifeSkills for Men

Also of Interest

9610

HOW A MAN

OVERCOMES DISAPPOINTMENT AND BURNOUT

DAVID B. HAWKINS, ROSS A. TUNNELL, III

DAVID HAZARD, *General Editor*

BETHANY HOUSE PUBLISHERS
MINNEAPOLIS, MINNESOTA 55438

Published by Bethany House Publishers
A Ministry of Bethany Fellowship, Inc.
11300 Hampshire Avenue South
Minneapolis, Minnesota 55438

Printed in the United States of America.

Library of Congress Cataloging-in-Publication Data

Hawkins, David, Dr.
    How a man overcomes disappointment and burnout / by David
B. Hawkins and Ross A. Tunnell III.
        p. cm. — (Lifeskills for men)
     ISBN 1–55661–941–3 (pbk.)
     1. Men—Psychology. 2. Men—Religious life. I. Tunnell,
Ross A. II. Title. III. Series.
HQ1090.H38   1997
646.7'0081—dc21
                                              97–4731
                                              CIP

DR. DAVID B. HAWKINS is Director of Pacific Psychological Associates in Longview, Washington. He received his Clinical Psychological training from Western Seminary. He is active in leading men's therapy groups.

ROSS A. TUNNELL, III has been involved in the men's movement for more than ten years. He has served as a seminary instructor, director of a private counseling service, and pastor of family ministries. He holds an M.Div. and Th.M. from Western Seminary and is owner of MacNificent Graphics.

Contents

Introduction

Why we wrote this book about men and struggle . . .

While I (*David*) am confident that he does not remember the incident, I first met Ross Tunnell in an early morning Old Testament Survey class that he taught at Western Conservative Baptist Seminary in 1983. I really did not want to take the class because I was there to learn about psychology. But to earn the psychology degree we were required to take the biblical classes. To my great surprise I liked the professor because he made the stories in the Old Testament come alive. He had a unique way of making the material applicable to everyday life.

I could not have guessed that seven years later we would meet again at a Bible conference where my wife and I were leading the worship. He was the guest speaker, and once again he brought life to the Scriptures. We became friends, compared notes and the life journeys we had both been on, and within a year we had sold our first manuscript. We have been sharing the journey and writing together ever since.

As a psychologist I see people suffering from emotional and spiritual pain in my office every day. It is from this experience that I am able to tell the stories that I write about.

However, it was not until I had to wrestle with my own issues that my writing took on less of an academic process. In 1990 my life was shattered when, at mid-life, I had to face my own burnout from workaholism and perfectionism, and learn about different paths to recovery. In a matter of a few months my life turned upside down. I did not know where to turn. I struggled to make sense of new painful feelings.

At that time I formed a men's group at my church (which Ross later joined), where several men in similar pain shared their various struggles and were "real" with one another. I had to face my own disappointments with life and search for peace as I had never done before. I took an honest and hard look at the different ways I had tried to live my life and realized they would no longer work for me. I grieved over the mistakes I had made and the wrong decisions I longed to correct. I came face-to-face with my limitations. Out of this turmoil and search for solutions, I have written part of this book.

The journey is not over for me. The struggles continue, though I have found some answers, and the Lord has guided me in the process. Where once I wanted Him to provide quick solutions, I now understand these will be few in coming. Through finding my own faith in Christ, which is ever grow-ing, I have come to understand myself in deeper ways as well. "The Serenity Prayer," which I share in chapter 11, has taken on new meaning. I hope you will enjoy the journey as you read the book and relate to some of the topics about disappoint-ment and burnout. Be assured that you are traveling with a friend who understands many of your same struggles.

For me (Ross), a turning point in my life occurred in Sep-tember of 1985, when, because of bad judgment and wrong choices, I found myself unemployed. One morning while I was mired down in self-pity, the phone rang.

"Hey, get dressed. I'm taking you to lunch."

It was George. A few minutes later he picked me up and drove to an outdoor cafe in the "artsy" quarter of the city.

While we ate lunch on the patio under a sun umbrella, George looked at me and said, "Ten years ago I suffered a personal meltdown." As he shared his story, I felt somewhat encouraged to know that I wasn't the Lone Ranger. My feelings of failure and inadequacy were normal given the situation I was in. He said his financial struggles were the greatest challenge of his life. When he was supposed to be at the peak of his game he struck out.

After lunch George took me to the Business Journal bookstore and bought me a book on becoming an entrepreneur. Next he took me to an exclusive men's store and bought me a $350 suit. He told me that if I was going to go out on interviews or in search of clients, I needed to look my best. And I did. Since that day George has continued to share with me and encourage me, and, next to my wife, he is my best friend.

That was ten years ago. Now I am back on my feet, and I want to help other men realize that though disappointment, burnout, and struggle are common, there are life skills we can learn that will help us through these difficult times and improve the quality of our lives. Feelings of disappointment and burnout have been my companion for too long, and yet I have been able to find support to help me use those struggles to enrich my life. I would like this book to be a "George" to as many men as possible.

1

How Did I Get There?

David Hawkins

"Steve, when are you going to get up and get with the program?" Sharon teased her husband. "C'mon, you can do it. My to-do list is so short this weekend." As she nudged him she sensed he really was not in a playful mood. For weeks—no, months—Steve had been nearly lethargic around the house.

"I'm not getting up for a while. This is my first day off in ten days, and I'm not about to tackle the garage. Your folks are just going to have to see the way we really live."

"What about Billy's soccer game?" Sharon persisted. "You know he wants you to take him."

"Why don't you drive him there, and I'll meet both of you at the field," Steve said, burying his head back under the pillow.

Sharon went back into the family room and thought about her conversation with Pastor Johnson the week before. She had been concerned that Steve was putting in so many hours at the lumberyard that he had little time left over for the family. But it was more than that—she sensed a deep discouragement in Steve. Her pleadings had fallen on deaf ears. All she received were more promises that as soon as the business was in the black he could cut back some. But they'd been having that conversation for the past five years.

As Steve lay in bed he thought about how restless his sleep had become. He felt tired a lot. He was also becoming resentful that Sharon could not understand his energy level and how *spread thin* he felt. After all, it wasn't as if he wanted to spend all those hours at work. If it were up to him, he wouldn't even be working at the lumberyard. That had been his father's idea. He never wanted a "career" in sending out orders for lumber. He had wanted to pursue electronics—but in the end Dad's pressuring had prevailed. Now he had so many years in this trade—plus a mortgage and a kid getting ready for college—that it seemed too late to make a career change.

The more Steve reflected on his conversation with Sharon, the more disappointed he felt. He'd been feeling burned out for a long time but didn't have any words to fit his feelings. He had never even told Sharon how much he disliked his job, or about all the inner tensions that had been growing within him. And he felt a little guilty for being frustrated, when other guys would love to have his good-paying job. He tried to fall back asleep in an attempt to escape the deadness that engulfed his waking hours.

Gabe

"What's up, Gabe?" asked Dr. Waters, his friend and personal physician. "Are you still pulling for the Blazers, or are you finally ready to jump ship?"

Gabe chuckled. "Yeah, I think they're going to surprise a few people. So, I take it you're still holding out for the Suns?"

"Absolutely," retorted the doctor. "So, has Donna sent you in here with your typical laundry list of problems? I seem to see you every five years or so. Is that about right?"

"Well, to be honest, Donna doesn't even know I'm here. I want to check out some things without her knowing. I probably sound like a million other people. I haven't been feeling like myself lately. I feel sluggish, tired, and more irritable than usual. Donna says I don't have the sex drive that I used to, and I suppose she's right. I don't have the same interest that I used to, but I just thought that it was a phase I was going through. . . . What do you think?"

"I'd like to get a broader picture of what's going on with you. Your concerns could stem from various physical problems, so why don't we run some tests to check that out first. But they can also be due to some emotional stresses. We may look in that direction, too. How long have you been feeling like this?"

"Oh, I don't know," Gabe said wearily. "Maybe six months. No, more like a year, I guess. It seems like time is going so slow. It may be longer or shorter. See, that's another thing. I can't think as clearly as I used to. Don't you have some pills that will help? Some vitamins maybe."

"Gabe," Dr. Waters said firmly, "as your friend I care about how your life is going. As your doctor I don't want you to suffer through anything. But I've known you long enough to know that you hold a lot inside. In order for us to get anywhere you've got to quit trying to be a silent hero. Let's go through this together, okay?"

Gabe and Dr. Waters spent the next half hour talking about his life. They explored his work life, marriage, and how he was taking care of himself physically.

Surprising to Gabe, he began to cry as he opened up and talked about how he felt. He had never sat with anyone whom he trusted enough to share the depths of his feelings. Though embarrassed, he had to admit that it felt good to get these feelings out in the open. He felt a tremendous sense of relief. Together they planned how to address his problems. They agreed to meet again in several days to begin some tests.

There are many men who feel just like Steve and Gabe. Lying in bed on their day off, they would rather continue to sleep than get up and face more responsibility at home. When their wives ask for intimacy (not sex), it often feels like another demand. It's not that life is *horrible*, because in fact it isn't. Life is . . . well, life. Work, kids, ball games, more work, meals, keeping the house in reasonable shape . . . and more work. They go to church on Sundays, but even that's lost the zing that it held years ago. Church now feels like another meeting, with its own obligations. Many men feel critical of their lives and wish they could trade with some other guy for a while.

Overnight, it seems, many men find themselves feeling disappointed and burned out. Trapped. Where were the road markers that could have warned us that we were veering off course? What happened to the altimeter that could have indicated we were losing altitude? Now everything seems foggy and it's hard to know what direction to turn. Everything seemed fine a few months ago. Or was that a few years ago? Time can become confusing. How long has it been since things felt "right"?

Confusion

Feelings. You can stop right there. Most men become very uncomfortable when they have to stop and focus on their feelings. And when they experience conflicting feelings, many sink beneath the waves of competing emotions that wash over them. Steve loves Sharon and Billy and likes being able to provide a good life for them. But he hates his dull job and feels there's no way back to the career he would have chosen if he hadn't given in to his dad's pressure. Sleep became his way of coping—his escape. For Gabe, the quick-fix he hoped for was a vitamin, or maybe a new workout regimen.

One of the most troubling emotions for any man is *confusion*. These are the times when we feel out of sorts, knowing that something is wrong, but with no idea what it might be. Most of us are not inclined to try to figure out this moodiness that engulfs us. We may attempt to deny it, but we know deep inside that these feelings will not go away. We may feel out of control, directionless, and in somewhat of a panic. We may want to reach out to others, but the effort is often just too difficult. Instead we carry on the facade that things are okay, talking with our buddies about sports, stocks, hunting, and politics. We cannot seem to find the ability to talk about the deep, personal issues. A quiet desperation can settle in.

Why is it so hard to open up?

One reason that men don't work their way out of the confusion of conflicting emotions is because we rationalize—that is, we justify the choices we've made because we don't want to admit we were partly right . . . and partly wrong. And maybe we don't want to face the hard work it will take to walk out of the disappointment and burnout we feel about our own lives.

Jim was like that when he came to see me one day. As he looked around my counseling office I could see his uneasiness. He told me, "I almost canceled because I'm not sure that my problems are any bigger than anyone else's, and someone else could probably use the time more than me." His *rationalization* hid the fear he held about talking about himself.

There was also the matter of the cost. "I can only come as long as the insurance pays for it." Apparently he felt that he did not need help badly enough to pay for it out of his own pocket. Too many men value a new set of golf clubs, or the rush they get when they buy their kid a new pair of $100 sport shoes, more than they value their own life.

In the first five minutes Jim acted like so many other men I had seen before him: afraid of his feelings, not knowing how to talk about himself, and fearful of the unknown. I sensed that Jim had at least one foot out the door before we had even started. One false move on my part would send him running. Because no man wants to feel "abnormal" in the eyes of another man, we rationalize our feelings away—or we run.

Jim related a few details of his life. Something was wrong— he felt emptiness, boredom, and anxiety. He felt driven and hard-pressed to perform at an unhappy job. He'd lost touch with any friends that he used to have due to the demands of his job and family. He was tired of trying to meet the needs of a wife who had been through emotional abuse as a child. All these things had been weighing Jim down year after year, yet he had never talked to anyone about them.

Then, a week before, he had awakened with a bolt, in a panic. In the dark of night he felt himself drowning in the depths of confusion, fear, and loneliness. How could his life have gone so wrong? Reluctantly, he'd decided to come and see if I could give him "a few things" that could get him back on track.

I told Jim I admired his courage for coming and sensed that it was difficult for him. I also told him that even though it's my profession to talk to people, there are many times when I feel awkward and unsure of my feelings as well. That seemed to ease his tension a bit.

Jim reluctantly agreed to return for another session—but he was clearly not committing to any long-term counseling. Like most men, Jim knew he needed to enter into a process of self-examination. But the problem is that we like to know what good something will do for us in very specific terms. Like taking our car to a mechanic, we want to know that things will run better after we plop down the check for services. If that's the way you're feeling as you read this book, I have to tell you up front: Your emotional and spiritual life is not as mechanical as your car. You have made many small choices and accommodations that got you where you are. It will take some new choices and consistent actions to help you rebuild a life of happiness, fulfillment, and contentment that you want.

In this book I want to help you get your bearings—take an honest look at where you are. Life has probably not turned out the way you planned it. You may have a desire to open up to others in a way quite different than you have in the past. You may sense a need to move in a new direction and yet not be sure which way to turn. This book will provide some answers—and more than that, it will help you assess how you reached a place of disappointment and burnout in the first place. It can help you to change.

You see, the way *through* is really the way in . . . *in* to discover once again who you really are and what God wants to do in your life. The way through is the path that takes you to the more authentic you that was gradually left behind.

Entering the Process

There is a common thread running through the stories of most men who feel disappointed and burned out by life. They awaken suddenly to "find" themselves in a place they never expected. They envisioned a life with a wife, two kids, a dog, and a great house as a "trophy" to their success. They thought they would fully enjoy the fruits of their labors. They imagined friends, fun, family, and financial success. Most feel as though they've taken an unplanned detour on the path to those golden dreams. Life feels as if it's come apart, when it should be coming together.

Believe it or not, you now stand on the verge of life-changing discoveries and opportunities—if you will enter fully into the process of change and growth.

Have you felt as if you're standing in the middle of your own life wondering how you got here? Do you feel lost, burned out, angry at the people who have let you down or demanded too much of you? Are you mad at yourself for missing opportunities? Are you mad at God for not helping you find the "right" way through the maze of life? If so, there is good news for you. This is a time in your life that has been called the "second time around." But this time you can learn about the rules—the real road map. During this difficult time you can review your life and the attitudes and values that have driven it. You will have the opportunity to see what has worked and what has not. You will gain strength as you take these important steps and make new and important changes in your life. Let's get going and see what can happen.

For Thought and Discussion

1. Is it difficult for you to admit you are disappointed, burned out, and confused about your situation in life? Have you gotten down on yourself for feeling this way?
2. In what areas of your life are you discouraged? Burned out?
3. Do you find yourself wishing that there were an easy way out of your particular difficulties? List several choices you can make today to begin the change process.
4. Have you considered talking with someone who could help you find a way out of your problems? If not, what's stopping you?

Dwindling Dreams, Vanishing Visions

Ross Tunnell

Do you remember when you were a child—wanting something very badly and not getting it?

For me there was a Christmas when I was up before anyone else and saw a new twenty-four-inch bicycle leaning on its kickstand next to the tree. The bicycle had been just the thing I had wanted, just the right color, and there it was waiting for me. Life, for that moment, was perfect. I remember wishing every morning could be Christmas morning.

But the day passed and life moved on. Every day could not be Christmas, and I had to learn to change my expectations. Life does not always give you exactly what you want—the perfect "gifts" that will thrill your heart. Life is, in fact, a mixture of good and bad, wins and losses, ups and downs.

The problem for many of us is that we have bought into various "sales pitches" that promise: If you do *this* you will have success and get what you want—every time. We have the mistaken idea that we can dream big dreams, arrange our life a certain way, pray the right prayers, work hard, do right—and life *will* turn out the way we want it. And lots of other men— from motivational hucksters on late-night TV to certain Christian preachers—guarantee us success and fulfillment . . . *if* we follow their formula.

But the problem is life doesn't always obey success formulas and principles. Some of us are *not* cut out to be managers or CEOs. Plans fail. People let us down.

Personally I learned to live by a set of spiritual principles. I thought they would guarantee my success as a man, a husband and father, and insulate me from life's disappointments. For instance, I believed that *being a Christian* was my first and biggest insurance policy against loss and disappointment. I studied the Scriptures and secretly felt that if I obeyed God the best I could, all would go well. Obedience would guarantee a no-major-troubles life. As you may be guessing, it did not take long for my dreams and illusions to crumble. That is not to say that the Lord has not been good to me. What I am saying is that my secret bargain with God—"I'll honor you, and you bless me"—was quickly unmasked. I had made a deal with God and expected great results to flow into my life. Some of my "rules to live by" were

- to be happily married—date only dedicated Christians and marry a virgin;
- to be successful in business—tithe;
- to raise problem-free children—discipline;
- to overcome obstacles—believe God's promises by faith.

How about you? Have you built your world view on these principles? Have you made some secret deals with God with certain expectations? Is there an unwritten contract that you have been holding God to? I built my plans and dreams on the foundation of "good performance." And since I was such a good Christian for God, I secretly expected that He would fulfill my hopes and dreams for me. I believed in God's best and fully expected to receive it. I determined that if I came reasonably close to following God's principles, then God would grant me the "desires of my heart." There could be no room for disappointment. What a great way to live!

Life has a way of exposing superficial answers to complex questions. Anyone over the age of thirty has most likely had some of their false hopes and "deals with God" exposed. How about you? What expectations have failed to hold up to the realities of life? Where have you had to face the fact that your relationship with God was not an insurance policy against difficulties coming your way? Dreams can dwindle like a slow leak, or they can vanish in one blowout.

Here are some common sources of disappointment and burnout.

Time Running Out

For many of us the dawn of disappointment can be pegged to the aging process. Maybe you have already begun to feel some changes in your body. You can deny it for only so long . . . and then reality talks to you very directly. How long do you last in a pick-up basketball game at the park? Does your church have a softball team—and can you still run the bases as you did at nineteen? It was a scary moment when I realized I could no longer defeat my boys in arm wrestling. I'm getting older, and my physical condition will never again be what it used to be. Racquetball with my teenage son is another honest measure of my aging processes. Realizing that we have less energy to give to our goals is a common trigger of discouragement. The emotional impact of getting older can also trigger a wiped-out kind of feeling such as Steve, the guy mentioned in chapter 1, experienced. Negative emotions, triggered by disappointment, can begin a vicious downward spiral. Not only do we sense time running out, but our vitality, too.

Jerry had to learn how to keep himself out of this spiral. After a successful career in city league softball, he shifted to becoming a player coach. He played less and less until he gave up playing altogether. Now he just coaches. The emotions he felt were nearly crippling sometimes, but he knew he had to make a transition. The guys teased him about the silver lining to his receding hairline. The jokes at times made him wince.

Where was his vigor and vitality? He did not like these twenty-year-olds teasing him about slowing down. Yet he tried to make the adjustment gracefully, looking for the challenges in his situation. He tried to put things in perspective. For every loss, there was a gain. While he did not have the stamina of the "kids," he focused on the fact that he had a lot more wisdom than they did, and he could use that wisdom in constructive ways. He even began to feel pride in his growing maturity. With every vanishing dream and dwindling vision, he focused instead on his gains in life wisdom. How about you? Where is your focus these days?

Family Matters

Some disappointments are not as easy to accept into your life. It came as a shock to my nervous system when my adult children made decisions that went against everything they had been taught. When our kids were small I remember sitting in church one Sunday, thanking God for my family. I thought we had some iron-clad guarantees: Because we were "good" and diligent Christian parents, we'd never experience major turmoils with our children.

We were wrong!

As my children approached adolescence I had a sense that these could be difficult years. "Difficult years" doesn't give justice to the struggles that our family has experienced. Those of you with teenagers in your home know what I mean. These young children, whom I thought were ours to shape and mold into the character of God, somehow decided they had other plans for their lives. I had thought that I would be in total control. Nobody warned me that these children would develop more persistence, tenacity, and downright stubbornness than I had ever imagined. I didn't agree to all of this when I signed up for parenthood. All of a sudden my wife and I are scrambling for books on raising children when we thought we had written the books. Can you relate?

There was nothing more disappointing than years of unanswered prayer for my children. I started praying for them before they were even born. I prayed for godly spouses for my kids. So what was I to do when I got a call from the police telling me they had picked up my son-in-law for domestic violence and my daughter was being taken to the emergency room? I found myself flooded with conflicting feelings about my daughter and son-in-law. How could these people, whom I loved so much, act this way? It did not make sense. Life was not fitting into the spiritual boxes I had created. Things were not turning out as I had originally planned.

Let's face it. We measure ourselves as men, in part, by how well we keep our family matters "in order." Failed or strained marriages, kids in rebellion or kids who fail to live up to potential—those can add greatly to our sense of disappointment in life. And if we have been at all diligent in our marriage and child-rearing efforts, when things mess up we can bear a huge sense of inner fatigue. After all, we've worked so hard—and for what? We tend to fixate *only* on the failures then, and not the gains.

Finances

Peter was born poor. He and his family lived on a small farm owned by a distant relative. His dad worked in town at the hardware store for near minimum wage, and his mom stayed home to work the farm. The four boys slept in the attic loft on mattresses on the floor. During the really hot summer nights, Peter would lie awake and dream about what it would be like to be rich. He figured he'd have to have his own business to make a lot of money.

Upon graduation from high school, Peter went to work at a local foundry. At union wages he was able to stash quite a bit of money away. He studied business opportunities and was waiting for just the right one. When he heard of the money to be made in precious metals, he became interested. After a lot of investigation and seeking counsel from those he thought were wise, Peter invested his money into silver-reclamation equipment. Extracting silver from used photographic and industrial chemicals was very profitable at first. The price of silver continued to climb. Peter was raking in a large profit.

Then the economy hit a recession—the price of silver went south, and Peter was no longer able to make money extracting silver. His company failed. He went bankrupt. He lost everything—his equipment, his house, his land. Everything.

"Why?" Peter asked. "I did everything by the book. I did the best I knew how." Almost as much as the financial blow, Peter felt that life had punched him at some deeper core level. He had believed so much in the value of hard work. It had been like a *formula for success* on which he'd staked his life: work hard; grab an opportunity; success is assumed.

Peter was smart enough, fortunately, to allow the catastrophe to challenge his beliefs. How about you? Have you staked your claim on certain formulas for success—or even basic stability? Have you believed that just being a good guy, a hard worker, or even a "producer" would insure job security or financial gain? Lots of us think that way, and we hardly know what to think when a career crashes or a company downsizes us out of their picture.

Life Is Not Like Sunday School

Most men I know still have trouble grabbing hold of the truth that life is not "fair."

Solomon said it this way: "I have seen something else under the sun: The race is not to the swift or the battle to the strong, nor does food come to the wise or wealth to the brilliant or favor to the learned; but time and chance happen to them all" (Ecclesiastes 9:11).

This guy, reputed to be one of the wisest men on earth, observed that things do not always go the way we think they should. We *think* the swift should win the race, right? The strong should win the battle, the wise should get the bread, the diligent worker should get the wealth, and men of ability should get the promotion. Right? "Should"—according to our view of how life "ought" to work. But if we listen and observe, we realize that our notion of "right and wrong" is itself a major cause of the disappointment that leads to our sense of deep soul burnout.

Let's take a look at what Solomon had to say after a long life of wrestling with these same issues.

Solomon mentions that *time and chance happen to us all.* That's the truth. Storms, tornadoes, and hurricanes destroy lives and property with no apparent reason. Or what would have become of Bill Gates if he were born in 1850? Electronically he was at the right place and the right time. In Peter's case, he started his business at the top of an economic cycle and there wasn't any indication that the bottom would just "happen" to drop out of the silver market, causing his financial meltdown. He took a chance at an unfortunate time, and he lost due to no fault of his own.

Is that how it is for you? Are you suffering for something that isn't your fault?

God Gives Meaning to Our Experiences

Fortunately we don't have to live as if life is only a random collection of chaotic circumstances. God can sometimes mix things up so that we learn to put our trust in Him, not in our own strengths, goals, and dreams. "Consider what God has done: Who can straighten what he has made crooked? When times are good, be happy; but when times are bad, consider; God has made the one as well as the other . . ." (Ecclesiastes 7:13–14).

Bill was standing at the fence at the Stanford University stadium watching his son compete in the discus throw. After tough competition his son won the NCAA championship in the discus. Just then Bill's wife drove up and said he needed to call their physician for an urgent message. The message was that Bill's recent biopsy showed signs of aggressive cancer, and he was to take nothing by mouth after midnight and report to the surgery ward at 6:30 the next morning! There it was—prosperity and adversity, side by side.

"In Prosperity Rejoice, in Adversity Consider"

Making days of prosperity and days of adversity is something God does. We can't change that fact. God does not leave us cold in our personal struggles. Yet He does need to coach us in the proper response. Crying *unfair* won't work! Essentially, Solomon tells us to learn how to accept and "roll with" the waves of prosperity and adversity that come side by side. Most of us have no problem with the prosperity part. But adversity throws us.

Solomon says, "It is better to go to a house of mourning than to go to a house of feasting, for death is the destiny of every man; the living should *take this to heart*" (Ecclesiastes 7:2). That is, *adversity pushes us to make heart-searching evaluations of our lives.* There is nothing like a funeral home to make one evaluate one's life and purpose to live better.

It is futile, however, to try to figure out *all* the reasons why adversity comes to us. It is enough to stop and consider the things of value, and then refocus on what matters. Many men who do this sense a new, deeper connection to God, as if He is saying, "Trust me, I know what I am doing in redirecting your life."

When we prosper apart from any effort on our part, or if we suffer adversity apart from any fault of our own, we do well to go back to God and put our trust in Him alone. Otherwise we tend to center both our successes and failures in our own efforts. And how many of us do this, never realizing the arrogance of thinking we have that much power over our lives? Without knowing it we mistakenly put ourselves in the place of God.

Ultimate Things

"He has also set eternity in the hearts of men; yet they cannot fathom what God had done from beginning to end"

(Ecclesiastes 3:11). God has placed in the heart of man the ca-
pability to appreciate and enjoy the eternal, and ultimately we
will not be satisfied with anything short of the eternal. Success
and accomplishment, as Solomon well knew, will not satisfy
the deepest longings of man. Solomon had accomplished what
others could only dream about. At the end of his entrepreneu-
rial exploits, he writes, "Yet when I surveyed all that my
hands had done and what I had toiled to achieve, everything
was meaningless, a chasing after the wind; nothing was gained
under the sun" (Ecclesiastes 2:11).

By design nothing in the world will ultimately satisfy. Our
first parents—Adam and Eve—for however long it lasted,
knew the joy of relationships without conflict in a world without thorns. Because of sin this all changed, leaving us with
only deep longings. This world is not our home. We are just
passing through; our citizenship is in heaven (Philippians
3:20). Businesses come and go, relationships work or break
apart—but our significance and meaning in life and the fulfillment of our deepest longings is found in God alone.

Have you tried to "make sense" of it all? Perhaps you've
found, after struggling for some time, that there are no simple
answers when your formulas have failed. I encourage you to
seek deeper in your disappointment, for deeper than answers
lie new purposes and directions.

As Don discovered.

Don

Don and his wife, Marlene, felt they were living out the
verse, "Hope deferred makes the heart sick" (Proverbs 13:12).
They knew their life would be complete if they could have a
baby. They had tried for more than ten years. Every month
there was the hope. Each time Marlene's period was late, expectations grew—only to be smashed again and again. Then
came the full battery of fertility checks. To further frustrate
Don, everything seemed okay. But Marlene never got pregnant.

Eventually, the strain of this disappointment killed their love life. They tried everything: herbs, acupuncture, fertility diets, even fertility pills. Nothing worked. Life was super-focused on "having a baby." Eventually they resigned themselves to thinking maybe God didn't want them to have a child. It was hard to accept, but believing God knew best, they proceeded with adoption requests. In the next three years they adopted two young boys. Caleb and Jared were an answer to their prayers. With the boys came the decision to quit trying. Spontaneity returned to their love and the tension in the bedroom was greatly reduced. Marlene felt fulfilled as she mothered her boys.

But Don's disappointment was deep. He struggled with the fact that he would never father a child. It bothered him, and he mentioned it often. He would ask himself, "Why can't I just let go of this and learn to live with it?"

Still, Don accepted this "redirection" with some peace. He loved "his" boys. As the boys got older Don spent more and more time with them. He liked sports and enjoyed coming to all their soccer games. It was special having his two boys play on the same team. They were both very good and were named to the all-state team their junior and senior years in high school. One day in Don's hearing, Fred (who had three boys) joked with Dave (who had three girls) saying, "It takes a real man to have boys!" Everyone laughed but Don. He felt only raw sorrow and a sense of loss. That is kind of how he felt—less than a real man. It was his sense of masculinity that suffered.

Later Marlene developed some internal problems, and the doctor recommended a hysterectomy. Don didn't realize how much he was still holding on to the hope of having their own children until he had to give his approval for the hysterectomy. He didn't hesitate as far as Marlene was concerned, as her well-being was more important than his slim hope of being a father. But it was just another in the long line of disappointments.

After surgery the doctor came out and said, "It is sure lucky that your wife never got pregnant. She had an enlarged artery attached to the side of the uterus. If she had gotten pregnant that artery would have stretched and burst. She would have bled to death before you could have gotten her to the hospital. As it was, we were lucky not to lose her. We caught the problem just in time and were able to suture the enlarged artery. She has lost a lot of blood, but the rest of the surgery went well, and she should be fine in a couple of days."

For the first time in thirty years, Don heard himself say, "Thank God Marlene never got pregnant."

In a way Don and Marlene were fortunate that they had a concrete reason "why" their dream never came about. In some measure they were even able to see why God may have mercifully protected them. But reality forces me to say there are lots of heartbroken people that still haven't a clue as to why their dreams have broken apart. Maybe you are one of them. The hard part is, in this life you and I may never have logical reasons to change our minds about loss or disappointment.

But we can learn something from Don's experience.

After considerable introspection, Don came to realize that he had been living with a very *self-centered perspective* on life. He had believed that he knew what was best for him and his wife. With this narrow perspective he became bitter when life did not go according to his plans. Could it be that you, too, have this kind of attitude and perspective? Have you formed a picture of what life "should" be—believing that your way must be "right"? Are you sure that you know what's best for you?

Perhaps the first step for you is to *surrender*. That is, to surrender all of your life, with its frustrations and losses, to God. He alone can redirect you even when you do not get specific "reasons" for disappointments in your life.

For most of us men, *letting go* is the hardest step we'll ever take.

But it's also the *best* step.

For Thought and Discussion

1. What hopes, dreams, and goals do you have that are still unrealized?
2. Have you experienced good and bad, side by side?
3. What good can adversity and disappointment play in your life?
4. Are you willing to place your whole life in God's hands, apparent losses and all? Are you willing to let go and let Him redirect your life?

3

Breakthrough Living

David Hawkins

Why is it that so many of us men are willing partners in our own demise?

In the previous chapter Ross looked at a few of the sources of disappointment and inner burnout that are beyond our control. In these cases letting go and letting God give us a new sense of direction for our lives is necessary to keep us from sinking.

But in other cases we have real complicity in creating our own meltdown. That was the case with Stan.

Stan was the one guy in town that everybody envied. I know I did. Everything seemed to come easy to him. He was sharp, not afraid to take risks, and seemed to be a real entrepreneur. Nothing was outside of his grasp. He must have read the book *Think and Grow Rich* fifty times, because his career and income had taken off like a rocket.

As Stan's business catapulted him toward success, he had to make some difficult decisions. Opportunities were coming at him at warp speed. Who would be so foolish as to let them go by? He began to sacrifice.

As time went on, Stan was fortunate enough to have a

spouse and family who saw the destructive path that his life was really taking. While there were some cosmetic changes that he made "for the sake of the family"—such as contracting to take his wife out for dinner every Friday night—there were certain things he simply did not want to hear. As the fights increased he became more secretive about his work habits. It was not long before he and his wife had an unspoken agreement not to talk about work. Tired of confronting him, his wife decided that she would just "cope" and bear it. Besides the high cost to his marriage, Stan began paying a high price in fatigue and irritability. He was on a one-way trip to burnout—and fast!

Stan even *knew* that his habit patterns were not healthy—but since he had gotten along this far without horrendous ramifications, why not go a little longer? "I can handle it," Stan grandiosely told himself.

The truth of the matter is that we usually *can* go a bit longer, when in fact we are grinding the gears inside us. Most of us can keep pushing, denying the damaging effects on our health, our families, our friendships, and our spiritual lives. Our wives will usually tolerate a little more, and the boss can hang in there with us a little longer. Our bodies may be screaming out for a change, but we can ignore the warning signs just a little bit longer. All the warnings do not work . . . unless something gives out. And in our blindness we say, "Hey, what did I do to deserve this?"

If you are like me, your ego and agenda can be much stronger than the yellow lights you're speeding through.

What—Me, a Workaholic?

My struggle was not unlike Stan's. I had the drive and determination to do something meaningful with my life. I had vision and lots of goals. Nothing wrong with that.

Enter the *problem*: *My* agenda and goals started to take over my life. Workaholism, like other addictive and compulsive problems, is only the symptom of deeper issues and root causes that need to be dealt with. For me, my need for *reassurance of my worth* kept driving me to further performance. The strokes I received from success fed me in an unhealthy way.

It was mid-life—being forty years old, with the decline of my energy and a sense of disconnectedness—that finally brought me to a crisis. Suddenly, almost overnight, I could not put in the hours anymore. I could not muster up the drive to keep the pace I had set for myself long ago. But the concept of giving up was as foreign to me as life on the moon. For a while I was a wreck. I wanted so badly to keep living the life I had set out for myself. I did not give up easily, as is true for most men. But all of that effort was to no avail. I had to have a physical breakdown before I could experience a *breakthrough*.

The cost to myself and my family was great. It usually is for those of us who tenaciously hang on to destructive, compulsive behaviors. I had lost many magic moments with my two young sons. I had lost a lot of possible quality time with my wife. I had looked for security in the enticing externals given by the world instead of being true to my spiritual values.

Are you the kind of guy who wants to keep going in spite of warning signs telling you to turn around? Perhaps you're saying that it isn't really so bad. There are ways to blame others to take the heat off ourselves—that may be a trick you've learned like many of us.

Not every guy can relate to driven-ness. At least not the obvious kind. While some guys get charged-up by stress and challenge and burnout, others wind up *fizzling out* because they are addicted to something else: *escapism*.

Sam

Sam was cut out of a different cloth than Stan or I. He was a rather passive guy who found relaxation in retreat and escape. He was not driven by the jewels of success. In fact, he was satisfied with simple things.

At first glance, when his wife called me for a consultation,

I could detect no real problem. I wondered aloud on the phone with her if it was not just a problem of things that *she* wanted that were different from what Sam wanted. I shared with her how common differing values are in marriage, and that it did not have to lead to serious problems.

But Sam had been through many different jobs over the years, never settling into a real career. It was not as if he had not provided for the family, she continued, but that his lack of desire to use all of his potential caused her to lose respect for him. There were many opportunities in his work, at church, and in the community where he could be more active and use his "gifts." But he was not motivated.

Sam spent the majority of his time in low-energy pursuits like watching television. She was convinced that he had low self-esteem and feared risking trying anything challenging. As a consequence, she felt that he chose not to try to improve himself. In spite of his good qualities, she feared her love for him would suffer if he did not make some changes. She asked if she could set up an appointment before things reached a crisis.

As I met with them I realized this woman had a legitimate concern. Sam was caught in a web of escapism, where he opted out of real living. While his wife wanted some zest in their marriage, he chose to avoid any demands on himself. I wondered what the origin of his avoidance might be. I could hear the pain that came from his wife's relationship to him.

Gradually I saw that Sam's questions about his own worth had driven him in the opposite direction Stan and I had taken. Afraid he would be proven a failure if he risked and lost, Sam chose to risk nothing. But in the end he was risking his marriage *and* his life.

Sensuality

In an attempt to cover disappointment with ourselves—fear that we are not worthy—many men turn to sensuality. They bury their fears in the conquest for a woman's acceptance and the heady feeling that "conquering" in bed brings them.

King David was a man who struggled in this way.

While David had many difficulties over the years, perhaps his greatest downfall came through his sensuality. David had a weakness for lusting after women. One woman was not enough; in fact, a harem of women was not enough for him.

One day David saw a woman who was the wife of one of his soldiers. His passion was out of control, and he plotted and schemed to have her—eventually plotting murder. With his life out of control, he frantically covered up his wrongs.

With concealment came David's undoing. Like David, our denial can maintain itself only so long—and then comes the breaking. In the Psalms, we read of David's unrest:

> "When I kept silent, my bones wasted away; through
> my groaning all day long.
> For day and night your hand was heavy upon me;
> my strength was sapped as in the heat of summer"
> (Psalm 32:3–4).

When Nathan the prophet finally came to the king, David was caught in his own web of deceit.

Fortunately, David's heart was still tender, and he confessed his sin, acknowledging his murderous and covetous heart. He was able to confess his sins and look at his true self, which allowed him to change.

David's restoration had begun. It took a breakdown for there to be a breakthrough!

The pursuit of sensuality did not fill David's inner need any more than it can fill yours or mine.

Power

Another man who experienced a powerful breakdown and an equally powerful breakthrough is Charles Colson.

Colson was a high-ranking official in the Nixon administration. He rose to the rank of Special Counsel. In political circles he was known as the "hatchet man." He possessed nearly unlimited power and yet thirsted for more. He could never get enough power and used his power unmercifully. Ultimately this thirst for power brought him to the center of the Watergate scandal, and then before the federal investigators. Finally he was convicted of criminal offenses and sent to prison.

It was in prison, denied of power, that Colson was contacted by a Christian businessman, Tom Phillips, who led him to surrender his ruined life to the Lord. At the lowest point in his life, the convicted Watergate conspirator experienced a radical change. Later he would say, "My greatest humiliation—being sent to prison—was the beginning of God's greatest use of my life. He chose the one experience in which I could not glory for His glory."

Colson went on to start Prison Fellowship Ministries and later received the Templeton Prize for Progress in Religion. But before his defeat could be turned to victory, Colson had to stop misusing power for his own ends.

How about you? Your life may never make headlines—but are you addicted to power? Has your narrow focus on getting *your own way* led to destruction of relationships? Have you crushed others in some way to get what you wanted?

Other Compulsions

In attempting to avoid the pain of disappointment, we men can slide into a whole array of compulsive traps.

Be careful here: Even though you have not lost a job, or your wife, you may still have a problem with compulsive behaviors. Work, sex, spending money, relationships, drugs and alcohol, hobbies—all can be consuming us, while leaving us empty.

Many men cannot relate to my powerlessness to overcome workaholism. But what's your area of weakness? What might you be using to fill the need in yourself—such as the need for self-respect, affirmation, love, and affection? Out of these empty places, and our innate hunger for God, we will often fill our lives with something that feels good temporarily but slowly breaks us down. What habit patterns are so strong that you find yourself *repeatedly* trying to give them up?

Whatever is feeding our particular habit pattern *can* change. We can courageously review our lives and face the real sources of our need. For most of us, it is *disappointment with ourselves.* Compulsive working, sex, drinking—much of what we do is a bid to feel that we are okay after all.

Laying It Down

So much of life has to do with laying things down. Said another way, it has to do with giving up control to God. That is not the mold out of which most of us have come. Research on men and women, such as *Men Are From Mars, Women Are From Venus*, by John Gray, suggests that men are action-oriented as opposed to being process-oriented. We are the hunters, the conquerors, not well-acquainted with surrender. Surrender—that word has a powerless, impotent sound to it. Who in the world wants to surrender?

In the film *Patton*, George C. Scott characterizes the legendary general who was obsessed with victory to the point that nothing else mattered. His cadre of men was a fighting machine. For Patton, surrender would equal *total disgrace.*

I wonder how much of that mentality you and I carry with us. How many of us still feel that we have something to prove? Men whose fathers were absent, physically or emotionally, feel a "hole in the soul" that they try to fill by achievement. Surrendering our pride so that we can admit our grief, loneliness, or compulsive behaviors is the beginning of healing.

This first "breakdown"—the surrendering of our facade— is the battle zone. Some men never have the guts to wrestle their ego to the ground and face themselves in truth.

How about you?

At Last, a Breakthrough!

In this chapter I've only touched on a few of the major compulsions that consume men's lives. I've done so to help you see where you may be using a substance or a pastime to cover up the pain of disappointment or burnout.

Please! If you have seen yourself in these few pages, get help. You don't have to become a 350-pound food addict, a divorced couch potato, or get picked up for DWI—you can be a man by taking the responsibility for yourself and your inner struggles *right now.* I recommend these simple steps:

(1) *Admit your problem to yourself.* Getting to the real root of your inner conflicts usually takes outside help. But you cannot get that help until you are willing to face yourself in the mirror and say, "I have a problem with . . ."

(2) *Tell someone else who can support you in your effort to change.* It's very easy to have a moment of insight and honesty—only to have the "General Patton" in you take command again. Too many guys have faced the truth one day, only to wake up the next morning with the thought, *I can handle this myself. I don't really need counseling after all. I'll just forget the whole thing.* The step between insight and *action* is a critical one. Find a friend who can help you get the right help—and who will hold you accountable to taking action!

(3) *Be willing to go deep. Deal with root problems, not just outward symptoms.* A lot of Christian men say, "Sure, I know what my 'root' problem is—it's sin." I would say that the fruit, or result, of a root problem is sin. But root problems are interior and emotional issues—even falsehoods we live by. And these root problems drive us to use sinful and out-of-balance behaviors in an attempt to solve inner issues.

For instance, a man may be brought up with the falsehood that he must maintain the upper hand at all times—total control—over his wife. If he cannot brow-beat, instruct, or force her into "submission," then he is not the manly head of his household. The result of such thinking is emotional, even physical, abuse. It means the destruction of any real intimacy and disappointment with marriage and women. For some men trained to "rule" in this heavy-handed manner, the sense of failure then leads to compulsive behaviors, and to other sins, because they have founded their idea of manhood on a lie to begin with.

Telling an overbearing, abusive man to stop dominating his wife, or telling a man who was raised to see himself as a worthless failure to go get a good job, will not help in the long run. True, he must change eventually. But he must be *helped to change*, and that requires doing the hard work of changing the inner attitudes that are fueling the outer behavior.

The same is true of the more common problem with us males. That is, we withdraw from our wives during times of inner stress. Why do we do that? Whatever the reason, it's a marriage killer.

(4) *Get help.* Don't talk about getting help. Don't just "pray about it." Get it! Find a counselor who will dive deep and stay down long with you! Do not believe the myth that habits that have developed over years will change with three or four visits to a counselor. Care enough about yourself, your life, and the people you love to make an investment in health that will last a long time.

(5) *Find the support and company of others who are open to honesty and change in their lives.* The world (and unfortunately the church, too) is full of people who are not ready to be honest about their needs, their weaknesses, their disappointments. Many men are scared to reveal their inner selves because they fear rejection or betrayal. Sometimes in Christian circles we think that discussing doctrines or church programs is all there is to "spiritual fellowship." There *is* more!

Do what you have to do to find a small group of men who want to work at growing in inner health.

(6) *Be ready to make changes.* As Ross noted in the last chapter, sometimes bad things just happen to us, creating disappointment, loss, and eventual burnout. Even if that's true

for you, the way out is to take the practical steps that will help you overcome in your situation. Staying stuck in passivity will not help.

If your compulsive habits have led you into a tough spot, you need to face up to your compulsiveness and find other ways to handle your root problems.

In either case, *change* is the order of the day. Not talking about it, not wishing for it, but doing the work of change, whatever that means for you. After figuring out root problems or needs or motives for your drives, you need to put a plan into action that will lead to *real* changes.

For Thought and Discussion

1. Are you a "General Patton" type—unwilling to "lay down" your campaign to prove yourself? Or are you a member of the "resistance," quietly escaping from disappointments and the pressures of life?
2. Do you find yourself drawn to one or more compulsive behaviors—even escapist habits—in an attempt to avoid the hard issues of your life?
3. What commitments will you make right now to seeking help and taking the steps to real, healthy change?

Disappointment at Work

Ross Tunnell

Few things are more important to the identity of a man than his job. We are asked very early in our lives what we want to be when we grow up. At each stage of development we're questioned about our future goals and interests. We look up to our dad and get a strong sense of the importance of his job, which clearly provides stability for the family. Our culture reinforces the importance of developing a career for ourselves.

Given this situation, it's little wonder that our relationship to our work dishes up huge helpings of pride, anxiety, and fear, as well as satisfaction. *Pride*, because we often feel we are doing the best job that we can do. Perhaps we're even fortunate enough to hold an "important" position. *Anxiety*, because we're never sure that our jobs are secure. What with downsizing and other inevitable changes, we are never sure that our feet are on solid ground. *Fear*, because in the worst case scenario the loss of our job can mean the loss of everything we've spent years accumulating. Or we feel *satisfaction* when all is going well, and our job fills our life with meaning, security, material possessions, and hope for the future.

But what if the source of so much of our identity is the

source of disappointment and burnout? What if we're fearful of downsizing, we've lost our job, or we feel stuck in a job with no future?

Let's look a little closer at some of the tensions we face concerning our jobs.

Loss of Job Security

What would you do if you lost your job? A frightening thought, isn't it? The U.S. Labor Department estimates that over the last fifteen years 43 million jobs have been eliminated. Even if you grant that those jobs were replaced by an equal number of jobs created, that's a lot of stress and anxiety for people caught in the country's economic transitions. In each case there are family members who are adversely affected.

With so much insecurity out there, many men live with a sense of impending doom. Companies use this insecurity to pressure men into giving more hours, accepting less pay, and putting up with deplorable conditions for fear of losing their jobs.

Take my friend Tom. He was recruited right out of college and served the firm brilliantly. As years went by he declined several job offers out of loyalty to "his company." Very quickly he had come to identify with his title and position, and the firm itself.

Married, with two children, Tom was a little concerned when he heard rumors that his company was experiencing financial difficulties. But he had been through some difficulties with the company before and had seen them pull through. When it was announced that a new CEO was selected to run the company, Tom hoped they would get back on track financially.

Talk about shock. . . . Not only did the company *not* get back on track and become more stable, but drastic changes occurred, creating instant chaos. Tom was one of several hundred employees terminated as a result of corporate downsizing. He couldn't believe it. He was angry, shocked, and felt betrayed. His "formula" for success (as we discussed in chapter 2) was destroyed overnight. He believed in the American way: work hard, be loyal, be faithful, be productive, and you will be rewarded accordingly. Job security was a matter of productivity. Somehow corporate America had changed the rules of the game. How could he be let go? He was the best!

"It is not a personal thing; it is strictly business," he was told. Regardless, Tom did take it personally. He had made a personal commitment to an impersonal economic machine where loyalty, faithfulness, and longevity apparently no longer mattered.

Tom was fortunate in that he got a severance package. While it held little emotional consolation, it was adequate to carry them for three months. After that, Tom either had to find a job or begin to liquidate assets. The way things stood, he could lose his home and his car. As important as his home and car were to him, he found himself thinking about his responsibility to provide for his family. They were looking to him. The house and car no longer had any intrinsic meaning to him, only the sense that they were signs of his ability to provide adequately for his family. After all, this is what he had been raised to do—that is, to be an adequate provider for his family. Now his basic identity felt up in the air. He was terrified.

Tom's story, unfortunately, is not uncommon. "Downsizing" or "reengineering" have become the code words for laying off thousands of employees. Behind the word "employees" are everyday human beings, with families and lives, hopes and dreams. Corporate explanations don't help if it's your job that's been restructured right out the door. Tom was fortunate to receive three months severance pay. Some employees are dumped with nothing.

It wasn't so long ago that when a company laid people off or had to let them go, it was an indication that they had done something wrong. It meant that management had messed up and corporate heads would roll. Not anymore. What once was a mark of ruthlessness is now a badge of courage. Wall Street seems to applaud the news of additional downsizing with a rise in all the significant economic indicators ("The Hit Men," *Newsweek*, February 26, 1996).

Call it what you will, "downsizing," "restructuring," "reengineering," "repositioning," or "schedule adjustments," it is still a shame, and people suffer. Men (and women) who lose their jobs suffer irreparably for a period of time. It is not easy to bounce back. Self-esteem suffers and bitterness and distrust sets in. Those that lose their jobs wonder if the next employer will be like this one. How long will this job last? The fear that is created is not easily dispelled. It is not easy to regain one's sense of confidence.

The "Golden Handcuffs"

With the threat of downsizing looming large in the minds of many men, a greater number hold on to jobs because of the sense of security they receive, not necessarily because they enjoy their position. When a man has a "secure" job and there are those knocking on the door who want his position, it becomes tempting to hold on tight. Motives for working at the company may gradually shift from a desire to work in that kind of profession to holding on to the job for dear life for the sake of a semblance of security.

Darrell has worked as an agent at a local insurance agency for some fifteen years. At first he enjoyed the job tremendously. It held a great deal of intellectual challenge, which fit his inquisitive personality. He was a people person, and he enjoyed the opportunity to help. During the first ten years he watched his earning power triple and his benefit package begin to take shape for his future.

Somewhere into his twelfth year, Darrell began to have different feelings about the job. He began to see a harshness toward employees and customers. Profits became more important than service. Numbers overruled compassion. Darrell could sense his attitude beginning to change. Where had the company's desire to serve people gone? Why was there such a push for productivity instead of realizing reasonable profits while still serving the public?

As Darrell discussed his situation with his wife, he felt a sense of discouragement. Here he was at age thirty-eight with one primary skill under his belt. He knew about insurance and how to sell it. He was earning a very respectable income due to the residuals he gained from long-term service to his clients. But it was clear that he no longer wanted to work in an industry that, in his perception, was becoming less concerned for the well-being of their clients. Besides, he was not sure that he might not be ready to try some new pursuits to keep from stagnating.

As he and his wife explored various options, they kept bumping into a wall. In *reality* he could not earn the same income starting out in a new field with a new company. He would lose the retirement benefits he would have had if he stayed with this company for another fifteen years. In short, he would be giving up a lot to make any kind of change. He felt stuck in what has been called "golden handcuffs."

The more Darrell thought about his options, the more certain he was that this company was not where he wanted to spend the next fifteen years. Every time he tried to rationalize that fifteen years was not that long, his heart sank. These were some of the best years of his life. He simply could not think of working for the next fifteen years in an environment that had lost its soul. But what could he do?

Perhaps you can relate to Darrell's dilemma. Have you wanted to make a career switch and yet felt constrained by "golden handcuffs"? Have you had a change of heart about your job and been unable to get back the enthusiasm you had when you first began?

What's clear is that you and I only go through this life once, and we are wise to consider the value of our time. For Darrell to make a good decision for himself, he needs to consider that he would be giving up another *fifth* of his life if he sacrificed the next fifteen years for the company and its benefits. Is his time and life *really* worth the retirement plan? That is a very personal question, of course. But it should be answered with a full awareness of the stakes.

Darrell decided that he would not make a rash decision. But he began to plant some seeds for a possible future change. He took a college class that helped him explore the nature of some of his strengths, some of which he had not been aware. He also took a workshop to learn some new computer skills. These simple steps helped to give him some hope that he would have other options available to him if he chose to make a career switch. His wife also joined their process to see how she could help create more options. Together they explored how they could pare down their lifestyle if they decided to make a significant change. The result of these few changes alone gave Darrell a sense of hope and possibility.

The All-Consuming Job

Another source of disappointment and burnout is the job that begins to consume your life. Some jobs, and some bosses, are like creeping fungus. They slowly take over your time, your energy—even your thoughts, as you are forced to think more and more about work, even in off-hours. A job can reach out and take over all aspects of a man's life if he is not careful.

Ted is an example of what can happen to a man when he lets his work consume him. As the clothes buyer for a large retail clothing store, he had enjoyed his work for a long time. Because of his passion for the work and a willingness to put in the extra hours, he'd risen in the company and in responsibility. While the job had forced him to move often to accept better positions with larger stores in the chain, this had been a part of the career he'd tolerated—at least until he started a family and needed more stability. Now their frequent moves became more disruptive and created hard feelings between him and his wife. His frequent road trips were soon met with resentment and the demand that he seek other work. He was beginning to feel the drain, too—but he'd invested so much of himself in his career that he could not even conceive of looking for a different line of work.

As things at home heated up, Ted became more resentful of his wife's pressuring. This was *his* career and identity that she was tampering with. What Ted could not see was the gradual erosion of their marriage, his isolation from any friends he'd once had, and his lack of groundedness in a church. In his case, his spiritual life declined and other problems developed. His once solid values began to weaken, he began to use alcohol, and he even questioned the value of marriage. His life was out of balance, and he was on a collision course for a major crisis. His wife saw these changes far better than Ted could see them. Repeatedly she tried to share her insights with him—but he was often defensive and protective of his world.

Perhaps you have been in Ted's shoes. Perhaps job demands have helped push your life out of balance, and you have changed in ways you do not like. Can you see a reflection in the mirror that does not please you? Your job doesn't have to consume you, and there is still time to make necessary changes before you experience an ultimate breakdown. It's very easy for our jobs to take on primary importance. It takes great inner strength to resist job and career pressure and instead build upon solid values. What about your family life, friends, and room for your Christian faith? This may take some changing, but the results are very worthwhile.

Ted learned, just in time, that his job was contributing to imbalance in his life. With the help of a friend he was able to rethink the ingredients of a broadly meaningful life. Few men have said on their deathbed that they wished they had given more time and energy to their work! Fortunately, Ted listened to his friend and the insightful words of his wife. He slowly began changing course and seeking balance in his life. He started looking more seriously at Christian values, the importance of family, and the necessity of rest and relaxation. While

he had long ignored these needs, he could see that he was going to have to begin to reintroduce them to his life.

Creating Inner Stability

In spite of all the turmoil and changes going on all around
us, it is our responsibility as adult men to manage our lives so
that we avoid catastrophe when possible. It is our responsibility to learn more about our inner nature and the things that
drive us so that we can be directed by healthy motives. Problems will come our way. But we can steer clear of total wipe-
outs by building stable lives based on a range of solid biblical
values. Remember: what we can buy or provide for the people
we love is not our greatest value. We are not money machines.
If we think that way, we are doomed to be slaves to our jobs,
the whims of corporations, or tyrannical bosses.

Ask yourself these questions:

(1) *How much of my life does my job consume?* Include the
time you spend commuting, evening and weekend hours you
spend planning, worrying, rethinking situations at work, surprise meetings, extra projects or hours that are "sprung" on
you. Include emotional energy you spend rehearsing conversations and irritable thoughts about your boss, co-workers,
and compensation. Include the time you may spend "proc-
essing" your job-related irritations with family and friends . . .
or time you spend bragging about accomplishments.

(2) *Do I carry worries about being muscled-out of a promotion, raise, or bonus—or even my job itself—by a co-worker
or competitor?* Most men are savvy enough to know it's a competitive world out there. But the real question is, do you know
when and how to turn off the worries and pay into some other
aspect of your life? Or do you *de-value* time spent with your
wife, kids, and other Christians as not important compared
with your work?

(3) *Do I hate my work, or some aspect of it?* Is your boss
miserable to work for—or so incompetent that you do the work

for him? If there is real grit in the gears at work, you will be ground down after some period of time.

(4) *What steps can I take to change the situation at work that's contributing to my disappointment and burnout?* If you are fearful of making changes, what are those fears that are holding you back?

Fear of losing something—our income, our home, a sense of importance due to our "rank" at work—is the hidden power that holds us all back from taking creative growth steps. The problem is we often hold on to jobs we've come to hate, or positions that are draining us, and become blind to the fact that the job we're clinging to is squeezing the life out of us.

Do you value your paycheck more than your inner peace? More than fulfillment? More than your *life*?

Be brave enough to do both the inner work and the outer work to change the things about your job that are draining you.

(5) *Who can help me to create a reasonable plan for change—whether it entails changes on my current job, or steps that could lead me to another job?*

If you are like most men, you may not be in a position to dictate terms to your employer. (Not unless you *want* a quick trip out the front door!) You would do well to seek the help of a wise counselor who can help you understand how and when to approach your employer to ask for changes. Many of us are too strong, or we lay down ultimatums, creating more conflict than we can resolve. Or we weaken and cave in to thinly veiled threats. The goal is to develop creative strategies to solve tensions at work—not to point out what a goof-off your boss is, or to sound as though you're merely whining about what's been asked of you. In short, the more positive and solution-oriented you are, the greater are your chances of resolving your problem a bit *and* showing yourself to be a valuable employee whose ideas deserve a fair hearing.

Every one of us needs help in creative strategizing, though. Get the sound advice of others to help balance out your thinking and come up with a creative plan for change.

If you decide you really need to move on from where you are, get the prayer support of your Christian brothers *and* the advice of a good career counselor to help you plot your next moves.

Your life is important. Your work matters to God. Value your contribution to the world through your work enough to spend your working days wisely, doing work that is deeply fulfilling to you . . . even if you have to make major changes to do it!*

We do not have to be so attached to our careers. We can learn to value and develop other aspects of our lives so that we are less vulnerable to job stress and career upheaval.

In particular, I want to challenge you to give attention to your spiritual gifts, commitments, and passions. Nothing can stabilize you more than living out of a core of strongly held spiritual values. Instead of being driven by practicality and the importance of earning a buck, perhaps it is time to listen to your spiritual side—to approach your sense of lifework from a different part of your nature. This takes a lot of work for all of us, make no mistake. But it is a major step on the path to a life of fulfillment rather than disappointment and burn-out.

One final consideration has to do with the matter of simplicity. To the degree that we have ordered our lives around the need to live within a certain lifestyle, we have limited our freedom. Many of us have reached a point where the dog is no longer wagging the tail, but the tail is wagging the dog. Our need for a certain lifestyle dictates what kind of job we will have and whether we will be forced to stay with a job we do not enjoy. All of a sudden the "soul" of our work is lost, and other so-called needs have become the driving force.

In light of this, many men have chosen to reduce their

*See *How A Man Resolves Conflict at Work*, by Paul Tomlinson (Bethany House Publishers).

debts and their responsibilities so that they are freer to make choices that are life-enhancing. Do you feel burdened down with responsibility? Would you like more simplicity in your life? This may be a time to take an honest inventory of your lifestyle to create more freedom for yourself.

For Thought and Discussion

1. How much of your self-esteem is determined by your job? How much of your security?
2. Do you feel ripped-off in some way at work? What can you do to right the situation? If you can do nothing, are you willing to make a change to get out of a demeaning situation?
3. What's your plan for making job changes or adjustments you need to make?
4. What are your spiritual passions, and how might they be part of a new job or career?
5. What are some ways to begin to simplify your life?

Mid-life ... and the "New" You

David Hawkins

On a morning run recently, a buddy told me that another middle-aged man had been diagnosed with terminal cancer. I was moved even though I did not know this man. He would be leaving a wife and three children behind. Of course, he did not expect this to happen to him and was not prepared for it.

What grabbed my attention most, I suppose, is that I am a middle-aged man. And it seems that all around me men are faced with ultimate choices and realities in the face of death and destiny. Vulnerability and mortality are concepts I had not given much thought to ten years ago. Now all of a sudden they hold new urgency. I am more aware of the clock and want to spend more time reviewing my life.

When we understand that the clock is ticking, many men feel pressure to reevaluate their lives. They can no longer take time for granted. They begin to wrestle with unreached goals. They regret missed chances. Roads not taken. Daniel Levinson, author of *The Seasons of a Man's Life*, says that in our mid-years, men need to look closely at their dreams and evaluate their lives from a new vantage point. Because we often want to achieve total success in our goals, anything less can feel like dismal failure. Often the gap between goal and reality seems too big—and the result is depression.

But for the Christian man, another option lies wide open. We can let God develop the undiscovered and undeveloped parts of ourselves and become the man God has designed us to be. For out of our mistakes and missed opportunities, God can refine us into the likeness of Christ—and help us discover who we *really are*, not who we think we *should be.*

What's Wrong?

Maybe you've read the previous chapters and have not seen yourself in any of the situations. Still you feel a big letdown. Many men wake up with a gnawing discomfort that something is wrong with their life. They've been at their job, or profession, for years. The days of quick promotions, rising salaries, and job excitement are behind them. "Been there, done that" seems to describe the monotony of life. All the fascination and wonder that used to be there is gone, and they are restless. Many men feel unduly tired at the end of the day and have little enthusiasm left to give to the company or at home. Thoughts of retirement begin to preoccupy their minds. They think, *Is this all there is?* Thoughts of quitting take over.

Maybe you're one of these guys. Your sense of disappointment is more attached to boredom than failure. Your burnout is more of a long-term "fizzle out."

I have heard it said that you cannot make it to age forty without experiencing some kind of burnout. There are simply too many opportunities for little disappointments and failures, for settling into deadening routines, and simply losing interest in the very thing you've given your energy to all these years.

Jeff was a forty-two-year-old computer programmer when he first began to feel unsettled. He had been at his job for over eighteen years and had been with a similar firm prior to his current position. Initially he had been excited about his line of work, and over the years he'd been a very responsible employee. He took his job seriously and made few mistakes. He had considered going back to school many times to advance his training, but working fifty hours a week for the company left little time or energy for such an undertaking. With three children, money was also tight. So he had remained in his current job and tried to accept his lot in life. But something stirring within could not be quieted. It was as if an undiscovered part of himself was trying to get his attention, one way or another.

Jeff's crisis came swiftly and unexpectedly—largely because he *thought* he'd been handling his disappointment, inner stress, and restlessness better than he had.

One evening Jeff came home from work, tired and discouraged as usual. Years of responsibility with little deep satisfaction had taken a toll on him. As he walked in the door that evening Janet said she wanted to talk to him. He could tell from the tone of her voice that something was terribly wrong. Janet asked Jeff to sit down as she proceeded to unload many years of feeling abandoned by him, and all the grief and pain that had caused her.

Stunned, he heard, "Jeff, we both know that things have not been right with us for many years. You haven't really been happy for years. When you come home at night, all we get is your gray mood. We see the happy part of you about once a year—when we're on vacation. I've decided that the kids and I are going to leave for a while to give you a chance to think things over. It doesn't mean the end of our relationship. That's not what I want. But we are no longer going to live the way that we have been living for the past ten years. I hope you can understand."

Jeff sat speechless. He was a long way from understanding. He felt overwhelmed by a variety of feelings, all the way from anger to hurt—but mostly *fear*. He did not want to lose his wife or his kids. He spent the next hour trying to talk Janet out of her decision, but it was to no avail. She had made up her mind. She reminded him that she had tried to talk to him many times before, but he had not always seen how serious things were. Janet told him that he had been preoccupied, insensitive to her feelings, and generally was not a pleasant man to be around. She tearfully told him that she did not know what else to do.

Both sat looking at each other, tears streaming down their faces. It was the first time Jeff had cried in years and years. Pent-up emotions that Jeff had squelched came flooding out.

Crisis or opportunity? That is what Jeff's pastor asked him at their meeting the next day. Which would it be? Jeff was still numb from what had happened the night before. When his pastor asked him how he was feeling, he had no idea. He was unable to differentiate his feelings, and all he could say was that he felt "upset." Most of his energy was focused on asking questions about why Janet would make this kind of rash decision.

Jeff's pastor tried to get him to see the depths of the problem. He knew change would not be easy, and Jeff would have to decide if he was willing to quit blaming his wife and take a tough look inside at his own actions and values.

"Jeff," his pastor challenged, "what do you think Janet is trying to say to you? What is it that's caused her so much pain that she would choose to move away from you?"

Jeff rationalized with his responses. "I know that I've worked too much—but I've been a good provider. There is no way to get ahead without putting out the effort. You know that. Someday I'll be able to spend more time with the family. If she could only be patient. . . . And I don't think it's *fair* to accuse me of being unhappy. I've never been a *bubbly* guy, and I think it's unfair for her to expect that of me."

His pastor sat quietly, wondering if Jeff was willing to look at himself honestly. Finally he broke the silence. "Jeff, you need to take a lot of time and think about what Janet is saying. I think she's seen a part of you that you have not been willing to face. I'd like to suggest that we meet again in a few days.

But between now and then I'd like you to reflect upon her complaints. In fact, I'd like you to spend some time every day in prayer. I want you to journal your thoughts and feelings. We can review it together when you come in next time."

How Open Are You to Change?

Are you at a point where you wish you could figure out *why* you feel discouraged, disappointed, or dumped on by life? Or why there seems to be nothing ahead for you but more years of "grinding it out"? Has your own gut been trying to get your attention—that feeling of general "grayness" that your life is not what you want? Or has your family been trying to wake you up to the truth about your condition—voicing their hurt, abandonment, or dissatisfaction?

Unfortunately most of us are hardheaded. But if we will risk stepping outside our defensiveness, we can begin to get new insights and begin life on a new path.

After several days Jeff began to ask what is perhaps the most difficult question any man can ask: "What is my part in this problem?" All of his defenses were screaming that this could not possibly be his "fault"—but he slowly began to see that this line of reasoning would not get him anywhere. Beneath the surface he had the nagging suspicion that Janet was right. And he had to force himself to admit that a stubborn pride had kept him from agreeing with Janet before. He did not want to say, even to the woman he loved, "You're right and I'm wrong." He really *knew* that things had not been right inside of him, and he had not really been happy. And at times he felt as if he were chasing some mysterious dream that he could not quite name.

Because Jeff let down his pride, his crisis began a *process of opportunity* for him. Slowly he began to identify his feelings. After several more visits his pastor suggested that therapy might be helpful for him. This felt like yet another attack on his ego and faltering sense of stability. Jeff reluctantly entered therapy, which was a huge step for him.

His Christian therapist told him that many feelings could come under the category of glad, sad, mad, and fear. Jeff had a tough time putting his thoughts into one of those categories. But as the weeks went by he was able to see that many parts of his life were not working. He had suppressed many feelings and had failed to share any of these unknown parts with Janet.

With counseling, Jeff realized that first of all he felt fear. Having been rather stoic for all those years, he had not realized the desperation and sense of isolation that he felt without her. He had built his life around his job, which was made up of superficial relationships. But those relationships—shallow as they were, combined with his family—were all that he had as far as connection. Now, without the support of his family, he felt very lonely and frightened. This was a new feeling for him.

Jeff had decided that the best way to cope with the empty time was to spend more time at his job. But he realized that more hours at the office was just a way to *avoid* feeling his fear, a way to keep from dealing with the places of his life that needed change. Rather than fill his life with busyness, Jeff was challenged to look at what was missing, and why he felt that he had to fill up his time with work. He slowly recognized that he had filled his life with productivity, drive, and ambition—not with a healthy relationship with himself or with others. His soul had dried up, leaving cracks where the depression had seeped in. Work was the only thing that gave him any semblance of fulfillment, and that had been disappearing over several years. He had futilely been trying to find happiness outside of himself, and now he knew he would have to go inward to find the empty spaces that God wanted to fill in with a new man.

Jeff spent more time exploring his feelings through journaling, and soon he came to see some patterns. He saw how literally empty his life had become. Jeff felt a deep remorse and fear about the state of his life. All he could see was a life in shreds.

Many men come to find, as did Jeff, that their inner lives are as barren as a moonscape. Some are bereft of a job with meaning. For many it's been a long time since they put any energy into friendships. It is hard for men to let themselves feel the grief or depression that lies just beneath the surface. Murray Stein writes in his book *In Mid-life:*

> "(A man) needs to identify the source of pain and then to put the past to rest by grieving, mourning, and burying it. But the nature of the loss needs to be understood and worked through before (he) can go on."

No Wasted Pieces

I was once part of a workshop in which we were asked to create a collage of our lives, hopes, and ambitions. We all set out on our task to create the scope of our lives out of magazine clippings. While initially quite skeptical of the process, I was won over after a while. If not therapeutic, it was at least fun. When the project neared completion the facilitator stopped us and made a surprising comment. She observed that we were all throwing our extra clippings away—saving only the parts of the magazine that we liked, that suited our purposes. She noted how much that was like real life where we are tempted to get rid of the junky pieces and keep only what is neat and tidy. "But the scraps," she reminded us, "are parts of yourself, too. In God's plan, nothing is discarded. 'All things work together for good for those who love the Lord.' "

Possibilities for Growth

For a long time we men have been controlled by forces outside ourselves. We have listened to what the world says we should be and do.

With disappointment and loss come opportunities to reevaluate our lives based upon an *internal* standard.

The man who is willing to face his isolation—a deep lone-liness that's been there all along—is the one who stands a chance of learning more about intimacy. He will find that he has actually been just as love-starved as his spouse. He is the one who can begin rebuilding relationships and forge stronger bonds to those whom he loves. He can learn how to commu-nicate and deal more effectively with those scary things called feelings.

Yes, logic needs to guide us. But we are guided in life, love, and work by *more than* logic. We can learn to let our true pas-sions guide us into career changes where necessary. The Scriptures tell us that work is good for us, but we must be will-ing to discover where our true gifts lie and pursue them. We can break out of old ruts and try something new and chal-lenging. This new sense of purpose creates excitement for us and for our family, too.

As Jeff spent the next several months soul-searching, he re-alized that Janet had been right all along. He had not been truly happy for years. He had been afraid to face that awful truth, afraid that if he openly admitted his pain he would feel even worse. While there is a little bit of truth to that statement, at least acknowledging pain can give empowerment to chang-ing things. That is exactly what Jeff set out to do. He took some classes on career transitions and how to match temperament with career. He found that he had been trying to force-fit a career to his personality, and that was not effective. It was like a light switch being thrown for him when he realized his unique talents, gifts, and passions, and he found some careers that could include them.

Jeff began to make changes in his career, which became very rewarding to him. It took a great deal of courage, but he reasoned there was little to lose at this point. His changes helped him to feel more self-confident, which then enabled him to make even greater changes. He not only faced fears but also found hidden strengths that he had never tested before. A positive cycle began to propel him forward, and he had the sense that he was finally tapping into the reason God had created him.

Giving Up the Ego

Someone has said that ego stands for "edging God out." Many of us have grown up hearing, "Do your own thing," and, "If it feels good, do it." This has led to "self-will run riot" for far too many. Christian maturity asks that we move beyond self-obsession and consider the deeper things of life. This includes letting the lives of others impact us. It includes seeing beyond the moment and gaining an eternal perspective. Materialism can give way to a spiritual point of view when we realize that possessions and thrills give only temporary satisfaction.

Moving beyond the *self-driven* aspects of your life is not easy. As Jeff and other men like him move through their crises, they come to realize that much good has come through their suffering. Suffering can be a refining fire. God will use these times to produce good fruit in us—if we will allow it. (See John 15 and James 1:2–4.)

We read in Hebrews that Christ "learned obedience from what he suffered" (Hebrews 5:8). The Scriptures are filled with the example of Christ emptying himself, setting aside His own desires for the sake of fulfilling God's purposes. Free from *self*, He was driven by a higher mission, by longer-term goals than what the temporal eye could see. He set His course from an inner authority that was not wrecked by disappointments or setbacks.

Have you been "edging God out"? Is it time to hand Him all the pieces of your life—the parts you like, as well as the scraps, to let Him show you the life design He is working on?

A Man Needs to Play *and* Pray

The more Janet shared her heart with Jeff, the more he realized that his life had been way out of sync. He had been taking life very seriously and had not been happy. He had secretly hoped that it was just something he was going through and that it would eventually pass. But as his counseling progressed, he realized that the problem indeed lay deep within him. He was in the wrong job, enduring a lifestyle devoid of meaning or fun, with emotional barriers that prevented anyone from meeting his deep needs for affection and companionship.

Upon further reflection he decided, as have many others, that it was time to rearrange his priorities. He decided that he was going to rediscover some of the old joys that had once filled his life and return to a saner way of living. He vowed that he would concentrate on developing an exercise program and a social outlet to get reconnected to some of his friends he had left behind. He also concentrated on his new career ideas.

He began to develop a greater ability for intimacy with Janet, and they made plans to get some marriage counseling.

Jeff also spent time looking at his spiritual life—looking especially for the undiscovered parts of himself that could be revealed through prayer. He found that what had been prescribed by others as "the right way to pray" was not working for him. He looked at some different forms of prayer that were richer and more meaningful than what he had been experiencing—silent, "listening prayer," for one.

Jeff was able to salvage his marriage and grow together with his wife in new ways. In fact, he and Janet began a "second" marriage, with new rules and expectations. Their relationship was free from many of the cumbersome trappings of their first marriage. They vowed that their relationship to each other, their children, and the Lord was most important to them. Careers were important, too—but not to the exclusion of their other priorities.

You, too, may be facing circumstances that seem unbearable. You may be going through a time of refining fire. Your marriage may be strained, or your job may be in jeopardy. You may just be sick and tired of being sick and tired. Can you catch a glimpse of the possibilities? Can you see that change requires growth and growth requires change?

Life requires many changes—but the rewards are worth the effort.

You must *want* to change.

You must be *willing* to change and be *intentional* about it.

You must seek out *change agents*, such as reading materials, growth groups, Bible studies, prayer, and counseling.

You must be *patient* and *thankful* for the changes that the Lord guides you through.

Most difficult for men, perhaps: We must learn to slow down and let God be God. We must listen for His voice and His leading and conviction in our lives.

The Lord wants you to be whole. *You can become whole.*

Mid-life and its challenges can present you with chances for change. It can place you at a high enough vantage point to look back and honestly assess what has not worked.

Will you listen to those who love you, and will you pick up the challenge and find the path of fulfillment God has designed for you?

If not now, *when*?

For Thought and Discussion

1. What have you learned about yourself from any struggles you have experienced recently?
2. What are the parts of yourself that you have kept buried or gradually left behind?
3. Read Philippians 2:5. What do you think about Jesus' act of setting aside His self-will? How does that relate to you?
4. List several goals for change. (You might want to begin a journal.) Tell someone about your goals for the purpose of accountability.
5. List your passions. What activities really excite you? How could they be used in a career or church work?

Causes of Burnout

David Hawkins

Mark had felt numb for a long time. He had attended a few Christian gatherings, hoping they would break down the wall that stood between him and others. When that failed to bring about the openness he wanted, he began to lose hope. All he felt was *detached*, and a sense of blandness filled his life. He hadn't always been like that, and exactly when it began was hard to pinpoint.

Mark was vice-president of a local bank. He had risen up in the ranks quickly, and his dedicated work ethic had been noticed and rewarded. He took his job very seriously and had done well, helping to turn a struggling bank around by increasing the bank's assets and client base. While it took long hours to make the necessary changes, he had made the bank a success and received a great many kudos from high-ranking members of the bank and community.

Mark's leadership skills had not gone unnoticed by others, as well. Given his high profile, he served on several local community agency boards and was chairman of the elder board, too. He provided solid guidance, made tough decisions, and could move a team in the necessary direction. He could make anything that he wanted of his life. In short, if he worked hard enough, he could go anywhere.

Where was *anywhere*? He was losing perspective.

For some time now, his secretary had encouraged him to take a vacation. It was unusual for her to make a recommendation like that. Not prone to comment on his personal life, she said he seemed to be enjoying his work less and needed some fun in his life for a change. Normally he would have dismissed her suggestion, but the same advice was coming with increased frequency from other people, as well. He was starting to notice and even feel self-conscious about his moods. He began second-guessing himself as to what could be wrong. He could not say that he really felt depressed. It was that he felt . . . *nothing*.

Unwittingly, Mark had created a perfect recipe for burnout for himself. He had entered the banking profession with high ambitions, somewhat perfectionistically. He had high goals for the bank and focused on nothing less than achieving those goals. He gave 110 percent and expected those around him to do the same.

At the beginning everything had gone well for Mark. He was young, possessed endless energy, and enjoyed all the elements of success. His wife enjoyed the early accomplishments, too, and the many benefits that came with her husband's success. How could she complain about a nice car, a house on the hill overlooking the city, and the many high-profile social engagements that filled their nights and weekends? Life was wonderful! Her satisfaction was another signal that he was succeeding.

Recipe for Burnout

Maybe your story is similar to Mark's. Or maybe not. Possibly you have been on a track—in your work, your marriage, or with personal habits—that feels more like a deepening rut than a run up the success ladder. Maybe you actually resent guys like Mark who seem to have the "Midas touch."

Whatever your external circumstances, most of us follow about the same "recipe" that leads to the deep soul-weariness we've been talking about.

Let's look at some of the ingredients:

A loss of satisfaction with what you are doing. At some point you left behind an enthusiasm for your work, your goals—maybe even your marriage and your family life. Maybe you rationalized, "It's unrealistic to be excited and fulfilled all the time. Life is full of duty, hard work, and commitment." But the *longing* for deep satisfaction remained.

A sense of detachment. When we lose satisfaction with our work, a sense of distance grows. The job we once embraced eagerly, we now push away from, at least in an inner sense. We tell ourselves that our distaste for what we're doing doesn't matter. But it *does.* And very soon it will begin to change the climate within—even though we can go on with the outward show. Some of us, oddly, detach from the things that do hold meaning and spend less time with friends, family, or hobbies. Seriousness moves in like an ominous thunder-cloud and we become overfocused on goals.

A lack of balance. As work, family, or church responsibilities consume all your time, other relationships start to slip into the background. Life consists of too much work and responsibility, and too little time is left for family and pursuing other interests. Interest in art and music, or sports and outdoor activities takes a backseat to business, though you promise yourself there will be plenty of time for that later. The relationships you foster are only maintained on a superficial level for the benefit of your work. They are shallow and may not provide for your need for closeness and honest sharing of gut-level feelings. Little time is given to nourish your inner life, and slowly your spirit dries up.

Another symptom of burnout—and also a cause of burnout—is *a failure to clearly define limits.* Because Mark was an excellent leader, he was often sought out by many to be on their boards and help to guide their organizations. He was often flattered at these requests for his expertise. He could sense their high expectations of him and didn't want to let them down.

When other people need us, we feel admired and invincible. Our egos swell just a bit. But our attachments to family and the broader support of others weaken with the increasing draw on our time and energy.

Not surprising with unrealistic demands and expectations of himself, life loses its counterbalancing recreative time. Eventually something is bound to collapse.

A sense of physical and emotional exhaustion. When you reach burnout, you've lost excitement about life itself—or the one thing that has taken over your life. Reaching social and financial success loses its luster if that's what you've been reaching for. You need more sleep and feel tired throughout the day. At times you may even feel as if the world is crashing in all around you.

Stages of Burnout

As you may have noticed with Mark—or perhaps in your own life—there can be a long, gradual phasing-in to burnout. It does not happen all at once. Let's look a little more closely at how it happens. Perhaps you will see some of the following dangers in your own life.

First comes *the promise.* You believe that if you work hard, perform well, and cover your bases, you will achieve goals, prove yourself, and find satisfaction. In short, you may think that attaining an exterior goal will help you achieve an internal goal, too. There is plenty of energy and many benefits to the focused and dedicated life. Even if we see our work as sacrifice, we give ourselves kudos for being so hardworking and selfless.

Next, at some point we experience *physical slowdown and emotional shutdown.* You may experience physical symptoms like fatigue, sleep problems, headaches, or stomach problems. You may know that things are not right. Someone—perhaps a spouse—begins to confront your behavior patterns. If you are striving excessively, growing more frustrated, then others are likely to notice your growing fatigue and disappointment. However, if you are singularly focused and highly motivated to get where you want to go, you will refuse to admit there is any problem. You may blame something outside of yourself—or someone else—for any problems you may be experiencing.

While we may deny limits, God, fortunately, made us with limitations. We cannot be God in spite of our heroic or grandiose efforts.

Ultimately then, *some kind of breakdown signals your burnout.* You may experience chronic fatigue, irritability, cynicism, depression, and anxiety. Your family life may suffer. You simply cannot continue to do what you have always done. Things are not okay anymore. It may take years to reach this point, but finally your body and mind and support system cannot take the pressure you have exerted upon them for so long.

The final stage—if you make the right moves—is *renewal.* Here you are able to find *a renewed sense of balance.* Out of the ashes of disappointment and burnout, you can gain valuable new insights that can help you develop a richer emotional and spiritual life.

This renewal stage begins when you are willing to take a long look at your deepest motivations—and count the cost of all that you have been willing to sacrifice to reach your goals.

Promises to *MySelf*

As men, we make promises to ourselves that shape the direction of our lives. These beliefs and ideals may not occupy much time in our consciousness, but they direct our lives nonetheless. What if some of those promises that we have made are not founded upon biblical principles—but are a reflection of ego? What if we're trying to live up to some standard that's impossible, and we've set unrealistic goals for ourselves? What if the standards we're trying to attain are actually not *ours* at all, but the standards of a ghost of the past—for example, a grandfather's dream for your father? Before you scoff at such a notion, consider the possibility that it could be true.

Mark's drive for achievement was shaped by his paternal grandparents, hopeless alcoholics who had done little with their lives. Alcohol had stolen much of their health and created an ongoing abusive environment in which Mark's father grew up. Though Mark's father spoke little about his unhappy childhood, he carried an unhappy sense that he had not achieved his full potential because of the abuse and neglect he had suffered.

While Mark's father was limited in his abilities to do more with his life, the expectation came through loud and clear that Mark and his two brothers were not to be limited in any way. In fact, the opportunities were created for them to have the best possible schooling, at great sacrifice to his parents. Mark felt an obligation to pursue a life far different than that of his father. The unspoken expectation underlying all this was: "You will achieve much and give 110 percent to make up for my limitations and to repay for my sacrifices." Mark made a promise to himself and set out to do just that.

Disappointment and burnout easily prey upon those who have great ambition, high goals, and an inner need for recognition. You will see more casualties among men whose motto is "Do it *right*, or don't do it at all." Perfectionism is the companion of the man headed for burnout. Focused, intense, with an unspoken mission from the past, these men often set out to achieve goals others could not achieve. They will provide for their own unmet emotional needs and attempt to do the same for other members of the family.

Maybe you've been the kind of guy who tenaciously refuses to quit because you are trying to quiet the restless, disappointed voices of the past. You may feel as though you have to give "it" all you've got, only to find out that "all you've got" is not enough. *It never is enough.* External accomplishments are never enough to fill the "hole in the soul," and you can feel as if you are trying to fill an endless pit using a garden trowel.

What you need is not a larger shovel, but healing from the inside out. What you need is to become clear about a more balanced and realistic set of goals that make healthy sense.

Are your goals *your* goals, or do they come from someone else? This can be a difficult question to resolve—but it may help you to set a new and rewarding direction for your life. A new direction that can carry you out of the trap of disappointment and burnout.

A Game Within a Game

Many men feel trapped once they've experienced burnout. Fortunately, they don't have to remain there. There is a way out. There are many options available to us.

I was impressed recently when I read the story of an NFL football player who had played for a string of mediocre teams throughout his professional career. The story told of his moving from one losing team to another. He was well aware that he had one chance at stardom, and yet he'd been stuck playing for teams where his talents were often lost. I can imagine that he'd spent years in training—from the ranks of youth football, to junior high, and on to varsity high school ball and college, he had outperformed others to reach the ranks of professional football. He had every reason to be depressed and consider himself a victim of unfortunate circumstances.

This guy was a prime candidate for burnout. He had been putting his all into an effort that never led to the rewards he'd expected. But he had decided to change his attitude about the game. He decided to play *a game within a game.* Instead of focusing on what hadn't worked out for him, he decided to concentrate on the areas he could control. While he could not control the win-loss records of the teams for whom he played, he *could* determine how he was going to play at his particular position. He remembered why he had gotten into the game in the first place—not for stardom but because he loved the game of football. While winning was fun and added to the enjoyment of the game, it was not the main reason he put the uniform on week after week. He reminded himself of the joys of the game itself and the passion he felt for it. He made a decision to play his position the best he could and let other things fall into place as they would.

In my neck of the woods, here in the Pacific Northwest, there are many men who feel the same level of frustration this football player felt. I know many millwrights, loggers, and crane operators who work for such behemoths as Weyerhaeuser, Longview Fibre, or Reynolds Corporation. They often feel their lives and careers are being dictated by others who don't know what they're doing, are not out on the "playing field," and have no concept about what is needed to play the game. These men often feel a sense of futility about their work. Putting their efforts into a job that is not going in the direction they believe is right, it does not take long to become bitter, disappointed, and discouraged. Do you know the feeling?

Most of us are filled with pride in what we do. If we've spent any time perfecting our trade, we know what we're doing. We want to excel, and we probably see ways for our companies to do better. But when we are removed from the key decision-making arenas, we begin to feel like cogs in the wheel. When we do not feel that our skills and reasoned opinions are fully utilized, we experience intense frustration. We become locked into a vicious cycle of frustration, anger, and irritability.

Unless you are going to make a job change, I recommend that you decide to step back and see the positive aspects of your job—to see the joy of the "game within the game." You owe it to yourself and to your family to decide *now* how to resolve your frustrations.

Changing Goals

Another powerful way to recharge drained batteries is to set more realistic goals. It is important to step back periodically and review the direction of your life and see if you are heading in the direction you want to go. True, we do have to make accommodations with reality. You may have set out to be a small business entrepreneur, only to discover that you hate all the pressure of organizing and administrating. There is no shame in finding out that you lack certain skills—few men have it all. After some reflection, you may learn you actually don't like the direction you chose. Reality *is* always different from our dreams and plans. And learning the art of accommodation is a tremendous life skill—also known as *healthy flexibility.*

So I ask again—is your life gratifying? Are you doing what you really want to be doing? Are your goals attainable, at a *reasonable* cost to you and your family?

This may take more inner strength than you think.

The world will gladly set a standard for you to follow. Madison Avenue will tell you that you should achieve a six-figure income, live in a 6,000-square-foot home, and drive a luxury car. "You *deserve* it," the world says. If you aim for these goals, you may attain them. There is only one catch—they don't tell you the cost. The cost for setting your goals so high is often the loss of your health and maybe even your family.

Even if your goals are not that stratospheric, consider whether or not they are realistic, or if they fit your real values.

Why not take time, if you haven't already, to list those things that are most important in your life. Place them in a priority ranking. Which are the most important to you? Which will give you lasting peace and well-being?

Now consider how your life matches up with those goals. Does anything need to be changed?

Get Support

For various reasons, many of us have decided that we *must* go it alone. We keep our feelings close to our chest and act as if nothing bothers us. We have to be pretty desperate before we'll seek out someone with whom to share our feelings. It's hard enough to ask for help in roofing our new garage, let alone share how *lonely* we feel!

The sense of isolation is a killer. God did not create us to be isolated men. We were made to lean on one another. We were created for intimacy. Intimacy has been defined as *"in to me see,"* and there is always the risk of vulnerability. But studies have long confirmed that being in deep and meaningful relationships with others is an antidote for burnout.

Another way that relationships help us is by creating a source of valuable feedback. We typically do not do well without someone to be a check valve on our activities and attitudes. We need someone who cares enough and has the courage to warn us when we are heading for the cliff, ready to self-destruct—even when we don't want to hear it. If we isolate ourselves, there will be no one there when we get too close to the edge. There may be no one there if we slip over the edge.

Ask yourself: *How am I doing in my relationships? Do I let people "in to me see"? Are there places where I can honestly admit my deepest needs?* If not, consider finding a friend with whom you can be real. It is crucial for your well-being and for creating a sense of wholeness.

Letting Go

Let's face it, underneath much of our disappointment and stress often lies a secret hunger for total control. We are not inclined to give up at anything. "Where there's a will, there's a way." Sometimes we need to take a step back and see that we may be winning inches in the battle but losing the war. We lose perspective.

Maybe you need to learn how to play on a team. This means sharing responsibilities with others. And maybe you need to quit trying to be all things to all people. Lower your sights a little and set realistic goals—to accept the reality that you cannot "have it all." The price for trying to have it all is too much, and the rewards are too little.

Consider letting go in areas where you are trying too hard, going at it alone, or doing it all yourself. If you will take some small steps in these directions you will notice great rewards.

Try it!

For Thought and Discussion

1. Do you feel a sense of numbness now? *Consider your true feelings.* Take your journal and note any feelings that surfaced as you read this chapter.
2. Looking at the recipe for burnout in this chapter, do you see any danger signs for you? Reading the stages of burnout, did you identify any signs that indicated you were already in a stage of burnout?
3. As you reflect upon your goals, is it possible you are driving yourself for someone else? Is it possible you are pushing yourself to meet some other emotional need?
4. How isolated are you in your relationship to others? Do you have a place where you can be "real"? What are some ways to decrease any isolation?

Strangers in the Night

David Hawkins

Perhaps in no area of our lives are the effects of deep disappointment and burnout felt more intensely than in the area of our sexuality. Because few men talk frankly with other men about their sex lives, we have little idea of what other men go through or how they handle problems.

While this chapter is not meant to be a "how-to" textbook, you need to know sexuality is a very basic part of your nature and cannot help but be affected by the way you conduct the rest of your life.

Though we briefly addressed the matter of sexual compulsivity in chapter three, sex is such a powerful force in a man's being, we need to discuss it again candidly.

Can you see yourself in any one of these three major difficulties?

Compulsive Sexuality

Often men find comfort from their deepest disappointments in compulsive sexuality.

Someone who has compulsive tendencies does not choose his actions but rather feels an intense need to satisfy his urges in order to release anxiety, frustration, anger, or sadness.

John is a hard-working car salesman in a large metropolitan city in the West. He started out in this profession as a way to be employed, but he soon found that he could make a decent living—and an even better living if he pushed himself. Actually, he discovered the first month that he did not need to push himself; the company would do plenty of that for him. He learned very quickly that there was a cutthroat quality to the work, and if quotas were not met he might find himself looking for another job.

John did exceptionally well at his job, as he had a natural ability to be persuasive and was able to get people to trust him. He found that he could be very successful—and as the company kept adding their expectations to his performance, he added his own to the list, as well. He wanted to reach the six-figure income bracket and to climb the corporate ladder. He could see a sales-manager position in his future if he kept selling the way he had been.

There were, unfortunately, many drawbacks to the car sales profession. He was required to work long hours and an erratic schedule. He had to make sales calls even on his "days off" and was asked to be available any time extra help was needed. His intense drive added to the erratic work schedule he maintained and made him a candidate for trouble. It was his wife who began calling John's attention to some problems she was beginning to see surface.

Kara was shocked the first time she went down to the car lot and found pornographic magazines in the employee lunchroom. It was more like a men's locker room than a professional sales office. When she asked John about the magazines, he felt guilty because of his spiritual commitments—but then he just shrugged and told her that it was no big deal. While Kara strongly disagreed, she let the issue die. What she didn't know was that John was leafing through these magazines during his break time and that he had secretly begun buying them for his use at home.

As for John, the more he worked, the more exhausted he became, and the more he used pornography as an outlet for his pent-up tensions. His secretive behavior escalated, and he bought more and more pornography, graduating to porno videos when Kara was going to go out for a long evening with her friends. He knew Kara would disapprove—and he also felt guilty—so he kept his "stash" hidden from her.

As time went by, John's habitual use of pornography began affecting him in ways he did not see. He told himself repeatedly that he was "normal" and that all the other men at the dealership were doing the same thing. It was a guy thing. He even convinced himself that many other Christian men were the same way but were just afraid to admit it. He kept thinking he wasn't hurting anyone. This kind of justification kept the problem growing

As time went on, John slowly changed. His spiritual values weakened, and his attitude hardened. His behavior toward his wife was also gradually changing. He was more critical of her and more sexually demanding. At first she was just annoyed and asked him to back off. Her response angered John, and he retaliated by calling her names.

"What's wrong with you?" John snipped. "You used to like it when I walked by and gave you a pinch. What's the big deal?"

"You're the one who's changed," she said. "You used to touch me in loving ways—not just when you wanted to get something from me. I don't like it when you walk by me and grab me all over."

John denied having any problem. He felt rejected and took her rebuff personally. He could not see any connection between viewing pornography and his cold sexualized behavior toward his wife. Nor could he see any connection between his long hours at work and their dwindling intimacy.

Over the next few months, John became more infatuated with pornography. He became interested in more explicit magazines, looking for "hard-core" material. He also became more sexually demanding of Kara. He slid into angry, negative moods if he was rejected sexually, and Kara found herself giving in just to end the cold war. But she was highly resentful of John's sexual advances when he persisted no matter what her mood. At times she felt like a prostitute.

John nursed his grudges and felt like he, too, was being cheated. What was so bad about wanting an active sexual relationship with his wife? He was only doing what other men were doing, he rationalized.

In truth, John was caught in a vicious cycle of ambition, tiredness, lust, and burnout. He sometimes had emotions running through him that he could not understand. He did not dare to talk to anyone about his sexual fantasies or his growing collection of pornography—no one in his church would ever understand such a problem. He felt trapped between feelings of shame and wanting to keep his desires a secret—and feelings of anger and justification that he was a normal man with healthy desires. From somewhere deep inside, however, he could feel himself losing control of his sexual actions.

Clearly John used sexuality—specifically, pornography and masturbation—as a tension reliever. Perhaps you can relate. Has compulsive sexuality, in whatever form, ever been a problem for you? Has your spouse ever complained about your sexual behavior? If so, your first step is perhaps the most difficult to take.

It is time to bring the problem out in the open. You see, shame cannot grow in the open light. It loses its tenacious grip when it's exposed. By finding one safe, trustworthy person you can discuss your problem with, you will be on your way to finding the freedom you long for.

Begin the process *now* of finding a good pastoral counselor or therapist who will help you address the real root problems beneath your sexual compulsions.

Also consider looking around for a men's support group that deals specifically with sexual issues. They are out there, and any addictions center or recovery program will know how to refer you to these types of confidential groups to help you overcome sexual problems. Many men suffer needlessly in silence when there is help, hope, and strength in meeting with others who struggle with the same problems.

Do not think you can escape the net of sexual compulsivity on your own.

Detached Sexuality

Daniel's sexual problem appeared much more benign than John's, but it created just as much havoc in his personal life.

Like so many others, Daniel slid into the habit of ignoring the true state of his marriage. But after one of their rather frequent sexual encounters, Daniel's wife, Patricia, got up the nerve to say something she had wanted to say for over a year. She hardly knew how to talk about their love life, even though they had been married for over fifteen years.

"Dan," she said quietly after making love that evening. "I'm not sure that this is the best time to talk, but I'm kind of bothered by something."

"Yeah, what's that?" he mumbled.

"Well, for some time now it seems that when we make love you're just going through the motions. It feels—mechanical. I don't feel like you're really making love to *me*. Is everything okay?"

Patricia's words caught Daniel off guard. Frankly, he was annoyed at first. He lay there quietly for a few moments—it seemed like an eternity to Patricia.

"That's a tough question," he said. "I think things are okay—but to tell you the truth, I don't know."

"You don't know *what*?" she asked patiently.

"I don't know what I'm *supposed* to be feeling. Sometimes I just feel kind of numb and don't feel anything. I don't think it has anything to do with you. I think it has to do with me and where I'm at these days."

Patricia turned away and started crying quietly. She wondered if Daniel still loved her, but she was not ready to ask that question quite yet.

The following evening she approached Daniel and asked if they could talk some more. While he was not terribly excited about it, Daniel knew it was important. They talked about how he had grown more distant since he had taken on more responsibility at the electrical parts company where he was a manager. As they reflected upon their situation, they were able to come up with several factors that were playing havoc on their sexual relationship. They made the following list, hoping it would help them find some solutions:

- Daniel was dissatisfied with his work and had never really talked to anyone about it. He was ready to try something new with his life and felt that he had some creative energies that were being wasted at his present job.
- Daniel had put so much of his energy into his work that he and Patricia had detached themselves from friends with whom they might have talked out personal issues. They had also quit talking with each other and felt that they were growing more distant from people in general and from each other in particular.
- Because Daniel had grown more detached, he had not been thinking about his relationship with Patricia. He had been taking her for granted. As a result he'd lost the fire of passion. Sex became a routine, not an intimate and fulfilling aspect of their relationship.
- The effects of Daniel's disappointment with his job was indeed being transferred to the rest of his life. *Nothing* held a lot of joy and excitement for him anymore.

Both Daniel and Patricia felt a little relieved by voicing the fact that his boredom had become a gray fog that had drifted over his entire life. Neither needed to feel guilty—they just needed to set out some solutions. Fortunately Daniel and Patricia were talking soon enough to correct the problem before it grew too huge to be rectified. They were both committed to their relationship and vowed to take corrective action immediately. Through their discussion, Daniel was able to see that his dissatisfaction at work had a lot to do with his numbness and detachment in the bedroom. He realized that he and Patricia would have to become more involved with each other to rekindle the intimacy in their love life. Both wanted to take steps necessary to light the fire again.

Together they agreed to attend a marriage-communication seminar because they wanted to stay in touch with each other's feelings, moods, and struggles. They agreed to begin treating each other with love and respect, knowing that this would create a loving atmosphere in which sexual feelings could grow. Though a little harder to do, they also agreed to discuss how their sexual relationship could become more exciting for both of them.

Finally, Daniel knew he had to make the effort to change the other areas of his life—such as work and exercise—that were causing so much boredom and fatigue.

No Sexual Desire

Kathy and Gary had a lot more work to do in their marriage than Daniel and Patricia. Their slide into emotional and physical detachment had gone on far longer, with neither being willing to bring up the topic. At the time of their first talk, Gary was no longer interested in sex. He was reluctant, as well, to even talk about it with Kathy. Consider how burnout and disappointment caused havoc in their sexual relationship.

Like so many others, Gary and Kathy had started out in their marriage with stars in their eyes and plenty of hormones to help the process. They could hardly wait to consummate their relationship, though they did manage to wait until marriage before having sex. From that day their sexual relationship had been wonderful, and both were very satisfied. Their sexual temperaments seemed compatible, their timing worked for both of them, and the sexual act seemed to be a genuine expression of their love for each other.

What changed? They both wondered how something so special had disappeared from their marriage as they sat across from the marriage counselor. Over time all sexual activity stopped.

Gary did not really want to go to counseling, but Kathy had given him an ultimatum. She had informed him that she could not live in a sexless marriage any longer. Feeling guilty for his lack of sexual desire, Gary had reluctantly agreed to go one time to a psychologist. He doubted that it would do any good at this point. He had lost his sexual feelings over a year ago, and his visit to a physician had failed to show up any physical problems for his lack of interest. He just didn't feel sexually aroused the way he had earlier in their relationship.

As Dr. Jackson talked to Gary during their first session, it was easy to see that he felt uncomfortable about the topic of sexuality—especially his lack of desire. With some resentment Gary agreed to talk about his feelings. As they explored the beginning of his waning sexual drive, Gary was relieved to hear that a large majority of men have sexual problems. He was not "abnormal."

As they talked through Gary's "sexual history," he commented that maybe his loss of drive had to do with his age—forty-three—and the natural changes that happen in a marriage. When Kathy said she didn't think it was a necessary part of aging to lose total sexual intimacy at his age, Gary bristled. Because of the tension in the air, Dr. Jackson felt it best to see Gary alone for one session prior to resuming marital counseling.

At their next appointment Dr. Jackson and Gary took a more thorough history of the problem, without the obvious tension that had enveloped their marital relationship as a result of his decreased interest in his wife sexually. Gary readily admitted that her attitude about his lack of desire had aggravated the problem, which made him feel even more inadequate. He had not wanted to lose his sexual desire.

As they explored Gary's history they discovered lifelong

habits of poor self-care, a driven perfectionism, and mild depression. Things had gone downhill fast when Gary found out he would not be getting the promotion at the TV station where he was a news producer. While he had told himself that it was okay, underneath that was not the truth. He had worked hard for years to reach his position and felt that he was the proper candidate for the promotion. Yet he had been passed by for someone from *outside* the company. Ever since then, he had been holding in a lot of disappointment, sadness, and rage. Because he did not talk about it, these stuffed feelings became a barrier between him and Kathy. His feelings of inadequacy on the job worsened as his preoccupation with his "failure" eroded his sexual desires. The more pressure Kathy put on him to "perform," the worse the problem became. He drifted further away from her, burying his feelings of inadequacy and guilt.

About halfway into their session Gary lowered his head and let the tears flow. He never imagined that his life was going to turn out this way. He *should* be general manager of the station by now—and he *should* be able to perform sexually. But he was not the manager, and he had no sexual desire. It was not until this moment that he saw how much he needed to express his feelings. He had been suffering in silence for a long time.

"Gary," Dr. Jackson asked, "have you voiced your frustrations to Kathy? Does she know what the loss of that promotion really meant to you? Does she know how pressured you feel about her sexual demands?"

"Well, I don't know," Gary replied. "I know we've fought about the sexual thing. I've told her to get off my back, if that's what you mean."

"No, that's *not* what I mean," Dr. Jackson said. "I'm talking about voicing your hurt and sadness and feelings of inadequacy. These kinds of problems strike at the very heart of what most of us feel it is to be a man."

"No, then. I guess we haven't really been on the same page.

All we've done is fight lately. It's been one power struggle after another. I feel terrible about depriving her of sex. That was never my intention."

As their session wound up, Gary and Dr. Jackson agreed that more reflection and dialogue needed to be done about the effect of the job expectations and loss. Gary had been carrying around a lot of toxic emotions. By seeing the connection between his emotions and his sexual frozenness, Gary felt some hope that things would work out. For once, he felt that seeking help was not only okay but it might even help solve some of his problems.

Are you at all like Gary in stuffing feelings that are uncomfortable? Do you have resentments that need to be addressed and "cleaned out"? Though men may be less aware of it, we are "hard wired" so that destructive feelings can ruin our physical health and destroy our sexual drive. Getting those inner tensions resolved is the way to restore both.

The Way In Is the Way Out

Toxic feelings of discouragement, failure, exhaustion, and anger do not just disappear. If not resolved directly, in a healthy way, they will wreak destruction. Unfortunately most of us men deal with our feelings by *not* really dealing with them.

In our first situation, John began having problems from his high-pressure job, with its high internal and external expectations. He dealt with these conflicting feelings by acting out *aggressions* through pornography and sexually exploiting his wife. Sexual gratification relieved some physical tensions, but it did not solve the real issues. Further, he did not connect his problems at home with his need to conquer at work, though they were very much related to each other.

As John's tensions mounted, his inner boundaries broke down. He gave in to temptation and ignored the warnings of his conscience. If the situation were allowed to progress without bringing John back to his real internal values, his acting out may have increased, possibly to further dominating and destructive behavior.

In our second situation, with Daniel and Patricia, we see how inner conflict played itself out in a different sexual pattern. Because of frustrations from his job and stifled creative energies, Daniel had begun to numb himself. While still in love with his wife, he had little passion to give back to their marriage. He, too, had buried his resentment, only to have it surface in his lack of passion for living and for Patricia. Daniel had *detached* himself from any sources of meaning, and his withdrawal had a damaging impact on his sexual relationship to his wife. His response to inner conflict was to keep performing—while his feelings just died. The disconnection between his heart and his head was wounding Patricia.

Finally, our last situation involved Gary, who was discouraged when he was overlooked for a much desired job promotion. His preoccupation with this "failure" stole his energy completely. From there the problem snowballed. He was not able to communicate effectively and work through his painful feelings. This was extremely difficult, especially since he did not understand the origin of his feelings. Talking with Dr. Jackson appeared to be a step in dealing with his feelings in an honest and clear manner. There appeared to be a lot of hope that his sexual desire could be restored after the marital communication improved as Gary learned to clean out his store of intense feelings related to his job.

My point is this: Our lives cannot be compartmentalized. We may not expect that disappointments in one area will affect other areas, but they do.

The task is to increase our awareness of how we are feeling, how our lives are going. We need to challenge ourselves to grow by facing our problems head on.

Healthy Sexuality Is More Than Sex

There are many tools that can be helpful in rebuilding the sexual relationship in a marriage. See if any of these tools may be useful to you in increasing intimacy, personal health, and marital growth. Explore and discuss them with your spouse.

- *"Safe Sexuality."* A marriage needs to be a safe place, where either party feels the freedom to say *yes* or *no* to sexual activities. Neither partner should have to fight or argue to protect their boundaries.
- *Mutuality.* A sexual relationship needs to be a mutually satisfying relationship. If the sexual activity is not agreeable to both, it should be stopped. This may include behaviors that don't appear to be harming our spouse, but in fact are—such as the use of pornography by one partner, or withholding sex as a "weapon" or means of manipulation to get our way in something.
- *Sensitivity.* Make the effort to *please* your wife. Find out what her desires are and attempt to meet them. Even harder for most men—learn how to tell your wife what you like, without expecting her to know or forcing your desires on her.
- *Non-demand touching.* Partners need to develop the ability to touch each other without it inevitably leading to sexual encounters.
- *Non-genital sexuality.* Spouses need to learn how to be intimate sexually without it leading to actual intercourse. Explore different pleasing ways to be sensual with each other.
- *Sexuality within the context of spiritual closeness.* Take the time to develop a close spiritual relationship. See your sexual relationship as partially spiritual in nature.

I have sought in this chapter to illustrate how disappointment and burnout will affect many different areas of your life—including your sexuality. While many of us men think we can compartmentalize our problems, this rarely works. The problems will inevitably have a negative effect on other areas of our lives. And if not addressed and dealt with properly, they only become amplified and cause greater damage. As the saying goes, "A feeling denied is *intensified*."

I am well aware that talking about sex is hard for many people. I hope you're able to face your life honestly so that you can get on with the task of growing and living. Change will not happen without intervention. Wishing, hoping, and praying *alone* will not change anything. We must act on our intentions.

Consider the possibility that you may need professional help if your inner stress has reached the point where it is interfering with your marital relationship.

There is no shame in seeking professional help.

A man is not a sexual machine. A man is a guy who learns to understand himself, his needs, and his own problems—and who takes charge of resolving the stresses and challenges of his life *before* they harm the ones he loves.

Be *that* kind of man.

For Thought and Discussion

1. With which story can you most closely relate? How does your story compare to those in this chapter?
2. Have your feelings of disappointment and burnout affected your sexuality? How do you see the connection?
3. What feedback have you received from your spouse regarding your sexual behavior?
4. Have you had a tendency to act in or act out? How has it expressed itself?
5. What are some steps that you are willing to take to improve the situation? Do you need to seek professional help at this point?

Spiritual Crash

Ross Tunnell

Greg is "burned-out" on church. He feels as if he gave it his all—but somehow he was never a "good enough" Christian. He got tired of feeling guilty all the time when Christianity promised to resolve his guilt. Why did his pastor—and almost every men's speaker who came through—use guilt to motivate men?

Tony was "into" his faith very strongly. He was taught to believe that if he obeyed certain scriptural principles, his life would be blessed. But his business failed. And when his kids became teenagers, relationship strains began to pull his family apart. Tony's pastor questioned him and said, "You know, Tony, if you had really been the biblical father and man you are supposed to be, you wouldn't be experiencing these problems. God holds you responsible for the failures in your family. Why don't you come clean and tell me about the secret sin in your life. In my book, when God removes His blessing, it's *always* because of some hidden sin. . . ." On top of the other problems, Tony was labeled a spiritual failure. He bottomed out and wanted to walk away from Christianity altogether.

Jim's problem is that whenever the pastor needs someone

to do anything, he calls Jim. After years of this, he's exhausted, resentful, and wants to quit.

Spiritual burnout is an unhappy secret rarely talked about in Christian circles. It can include many negative feelings about God—even a questioning of whether or not God cares about us or even exists. Issues that had previously been resolved may rear their heads again. It is not uncommon to feel useless to God and to feel a great chasm between yourself and God. Try as you might to do the mechanics to build a bridge to God, you may only feel His absence. A deep void. This is evidenced by the fact that church is the last place you want to be. This can be a terribly difficult time of emptiness and isolation. It is made worse if you try to "fake it" with your Christian friends.

Complicating matters, beneath your sense of burnout may lie feelings of shame and embarrassment. Knowing you are *pretending* to be alive spiritually when you really feel dead is a hard act to live with. Playing a role is draining and cannot last forever. Spiritual burnout can come as part of emotional burnout. We cannot separate our physical, emotional, and spiritual natures, and sometimes a long string of disappointments in our spiritually based relationships can ultimately wipe us out. Men who work or even volunteer in churches and ministries can feel so disappointed in the pettiness, falseness, and backbiting of other Christians that it wears down their core trust in the Word of God—maybe even in God himself. *How can Christianity be true*, they ask themselves privately, *when Christians can be so much like non-Christians—so mean and selfish?*

If this question has been eating your soul alive, it's time to get it out in the open and deal with it. You need to find a good spiritual counselor who will allow you to be honest—and who will challenge you to grow and dig in your own faith, not simply trash the faith because of the mistakes and sins of others, and not wallow in cynicism.

Losing the Ball and Chain

Guilt is another major source of spiritual burnout. Few things weigh more heavily on a man's soul than a guilty conscience.

David said, "My guilt has overwhelmed me like a burden too heavy to bear" (Psalm 38:4). What happens to a man overburdened with guilt?

Consider the story of one guy I met in a lockup unit at a hospital.

I was visiting at St. Joseph's when a man in hospital scrubs approached me. "Are you a reverend?" he asked, knowing that I was making a round of hospital calls.

"No," I said, "but I do attend church."

"That's good enough. Please come with me." I was curious as he led me into a room where a man was being forced into a straitjacket by two orderlies. The man was screaming, "I want to see a reverend. Won't someone help me? I'm a Christian—I want to see a reverend."

The orderly shouted, "Here is someone to talk to you." And he literally pushed me forward. I introduced myself and told him, "I attend church."

"My name is Scott, and I'm a Christian," he said in a panicked voice. "Why is this happening to me? Why is God allowing this to happen? I can't do anything right. My life is out of control. I can't keep a job. Every little thing sets me off. I got so bad, my wife had me picked up and dropped off here."

"Why are they tying you down?" I asked.

"Because I tried to hurt myself," he muttered as he dropped his head.

Scott was obviously a very troubled person. As we were left alone to talk, he calmed down. It was odd talking with a guy in a straitjacket.

He told me a little about his life and all the things that pushed his buttons the wrong way. He was not on drugs and had no history of mental or emotional disorders. He was physically healthy. He was married, with two teenage children. But he had become so jumpy that he wasn't able to keep a steady job, and his wife was hosting Tupperware® parties to keep the lights on.

One question I asked brought a curious look to his eye: "Do you know of anything that is wrong about your life—I mean, is there something you've done wrong?"

"What do you mean?" he asked.

"I mean, are you *doing* anything that you know is wrong? Do you have any secret sin in your life you're not being honest about?"

He looked off in a haze. Then, slowly, he said, "I can't think of anything."

"Think about it," I said. "Remember anything that comes to mind, and we'll talk about it when I stop by tomorrow to see how you're doing."

"You'll come back?" he asked, looking relieved.

"Of course."

The next day when I arrived, he was sitting up in bed. The straitjacket was gone, and he was joking with the nurse. "You look a hundred percent better today, Scott," I ventured.

"You know that question you asked me about secret sin? Well, I've been working on it." He pulled out several pieces of paper with scribbling all over them and started reading. "Five years ago I cheated on my wife, but I never told her. I haven't paid income taxes for over twelve years. . . ." He paused and looked up, smiling. "Is that the sort of thing you're looking for?"

I tried not to laugh. "That's a pretty good start."

Scott had two and a half pages of things he'd done that were definitely wrong. Even though he'd become a Christian, he'd never made any of them right. Somehow a bolt of inspiration had helped me hit the proverbial nail on the head. Guilt, like a cancer, had spread through much of his life, and as it appeared, the resulting inner tension had pushed him over the edge.

My suggestion was to start at the top—the big ones first.

"Taxes—we'll tackle taxes first. As soon as you're able, we'll go down to the local IRS office and take care of those back taxes."

"What if they lock me up?" Scott worried.

"It's better to be locked up on the outside and free on the inside. Isn't it?" I challenged. "After all, when you were locked up on the inside, you wound up in a straitjacket."

The week Scott got out of the hospital we trucked on down to the IRS, where he was assigned an agent who handled collections. No nets dropped on Scott from the ceiling. He wasn't whisked off to jail. It was fairly routine. The agent gave us all the back forms we needed and suggested we get a tax professional to help us fill them out.

We found a CPA in our church who helped, and eventually we were able to get all the forms filled out and filed.

The interesting thing is that the CPA later hired Scott to be his bill collector. Scott knew all the excuses and had compassion on those he called on because he knew exactly how they felt. Those people ended up paying him *first* because he was so understanding. Scott became the firm's best collector!

Scott's story illustrates Proverbs 28:13, "He who conceals his sins does not prosper, but whoever confesses and renounces them finds mercy." Scott was willing to forsake his wrongdoing and to make things right, and as a result he regained the freedom of a clear conscience. Most of Scott's guilt was legitimate—he earned it. And by seeking God's forgiveness and working to restore his debts, he regained inner stability.

While Scott's true story may seem somewhat extreme to you, it illustrates how guilt can weigh down the soul and erode a man's well-being from the inside out. The task I assigned to Scott was quite similar to one of the steps in the Twelve-Step Program of Alcoholics Anonymous. In that program, members are asked to list all the persons they have harmed and be prepared to make amends to all wherever possible. The purpose for this assignment is for the cleansing of the conscience, which can have profound effects on our emotional well-being. Your recovery from burnout could be greatly enhanced by doing a similar "inventory."

A cleansing of the soul *can* lead to dramatic results.

Rationalizing

Pop psychology says, "Follow the dictates of your own conscience." This is good advice if you have a good conscience. But what if you don't have a good conscience? What if it is miseducated? What if it is scarred? Then "Let your conscience be your guide" is not good advice. Unfortunately many men have learned to rationalize behavior that's wrong, hurtful, and a sin in God's eyes. They have learned how to justify what they're doing—that is, they come up with twisted explanations to make it *sound* right. But they are searing their soul and causing spiritual burnout.

Yes, it is possible to have our consciences miseducated. Put another way, it is possible to feel bad about things we shouldn't feel bad about and feel good about things we shouldn't feel good about.

Ben conducts his business on a barter or cash-only basis. He openly states he doesn't want a paper trail for the IRS to follow and find out how much he really earns. He has made himself believe he's being "resourceful" and "smart." Ben has talked himself into believing he is doing the right thing. He has "educated" his conscience, so to speak, to affirm his behavior.

Justification and rationalization are two of the best anesthetics for a guilty conscience. Have you heard any of these phrases—used any of these justifications?

"I owe it to myself."

"He has too much money anyway."

"What he doesn't know won't hurt him."

"The company won't even miss it."

"Everybody is doing it."

"I had to do it if I was ever going to get ahead."

"It felt like the right thing to do."

"It's easier to ask forgiveness than to ask permission."

"The government would just spend it in ungodly ways anyway."

Can you identify with any of these rationalizations for wrong behavior? When you step over the line in small ways, do you have a standard line that you use to make things seem all right?

If our conscience can be miseducated, it can be reeducated. That is best done by Bible study. "How can a . . . man keep his way pure? By living according to [God's] word" (Psalm 119:9). In order to do the right thing we need to *know* what the right thing is. We need an objective standard that's outside our self-centered beings to measure and evaluate right and wrong. Otherwise we will all do what is right in our own eyes, with disastrous consequences. "There is a way that seems right to a man, but in the end it leads to death" (Proverbs 14:12).

Another way to properly educate our conscience is to associate with people who know and do right: "He who walks with the wise grows wise" (Proverbs 13:20). And the opposite is also true: "Bad company corrupts good character" (1 Corinthians 15:33). For the man who wants to practice the truth and maintain a clear conscience, it is very important who he hangs out with. Joining a men's Bible study or a men's growth or accountability group helps us make righteousness, faith, and godly love a part of our lives.

The best way to prevent the weight of a guilty conscience is to *avoid* violating your conscience in the first place. If you have violated your conscience, there are several things you need to do to restore health to your conscience. The first is to repent and confess your wrong to God, for He's the one to whom you must ultimately answer. Then you need to make it right with the one(s) involved and make restitution wherever possible.

As Paul said, "I strive always to keep my conscience clear before God and man" (Acts 24:16). A good conscience and sincere faith are essential ingredients for health and growth in the spiritual life.

False Guilt

Richard often complained about his love life. Whenever he talked about it, he always would say he let the best one get away. One phrase he used repeatedly was, "I can't forgive myself."

I asked Richard to explain what he meant by not being "able" to forgive himself.

The incident he was referring to happened during college. He had been involved with an on-campus Christian group. Each year during summer vacation, hundreds of campus workers would come to organizational headquarters for more training, encouragement, and planning for the next year of campus ministry.

In the summer of his junior year, Richard met Sandy. If ever there was love at first sight, this was it. They had so much in common—similar family backgrounds, and mostly a strong desire to serve the Lord. They did their summer assignments together, and one assignment was beach evangelism. They walked the beach sharing their faith with various sunbathers. Toward evening they had dinner in a nice restaurant overlooking Paradise Cove. Afterward they walked back along the beach. It was a balmy evening, and a full moon rose over the surf. It was a "perfect" evening. Sandy resisted Richard's advances at first, but he persisted and finally chemistry took over. Before they knew it they were sexually involved.

The next day Richard felt terrible. He prayed and asked God to forgive him. He found Sandy and confessed to her how wrong he had been. They asked for, and granted each other, forgiveness. Sandy told her dorm supervisor about her indiscretion and was told not to be alone with Richard the remainder of her stay at headquarters. They complied with that rule, and their relationship quickly wilted and died. Sandy really did not want to see him again.

Now Richard said he felt forgiven by Sandy and God—but he couldn't forgive himself, though ten years had passed. "I've ruined my one chance at love."

Richard's inability or unwillingness to forgive himself fascinated me. If anything, I am too easy on myself. I find it all too easy to forgive myself and overlook my faults and sins. So why does a guy like Richard feel he can't forgive himself?

Matthew 18 is clear enough: If I have accepted God's forgiveness of my enormous debt to Him, *I am forgiven*. Based on that—how dare I not forgive my brother his small offense to me? By forgiving others I demonstrate that I have truly understood the enormous love and forgiveness of God—so much that I can offer it to others.

The same must be true when it comes to forgiving myself.

In trying to understand *self-forgiveness* I have wrestled with David's statement, "Against you, you only [God], have I sinned and done what is evil in your sight" (Psalm 51:4). Think about it. David had just been confronted by Nathan the prophet about his sin with Bathsheba. David lusted for Bathsheba, had sex with her, got her pregnant, tried to pass off the pregnancy on her husband by lying to him—then he eventually had the man killed to cover his evil action. In a great gesture of magnanimity, he then took the widowed Bathsheba into his home for protective custody. *Give me a break!* How could David say to God, "Against you, you only, have I sinned"?

The answer lies in the reply to this question: *Who made the rules?* Who said, "Thou shalt not kill"? Who said, "Thou shalt not commit adultery"? Was it David who said, "Thou shalt not lie"? Was it Bathsheba who said, "Thou shall not covet another man's wife"? These are God's rules, and David broke them. So David was right that his sin was primarily against God and God only. For at the bottom of every man's sin—David's, yours, and mine—lies a blatant disregard and despising of the authority of God, our soul's true Father.

Asking for and granting forgiveness is the appropriate

method for restoring a relationship that has been broken by sin. Is there a possibility of sinning against one's *self*? The apostle Paul seems to say *yes*: "All other sins a man commits are outside his body, but he who sins sexually sins against his own body" (1 Corinthians 6:18). Maybe it is possible to sin against yourself—but that still doesn't mean you can't forgive yourself. Since the blood of Jesus Christ "cleanses from all sin," doesn't that mean *all* sin?

In talking with Richard, another subject intruded into our conversation. *Repentance.*

Repentance comes before asking and receiving forgiveness. A repentant attitude means that you have truly seen the wrong you have done, the damage you have caused, and you want to change your actions so the wrong will not occur again. You take full responsibility for your behavior upon yourself. When you are willing to head in a new direction, you begin to escape that *"I can't forgive myself"* feeling that feeds guilt and spiritual burnout. More than that, you also restore relationships on a right footing.

Picture this: While driving to church one Sunday morning, I say something hurtful to my wife, and she starts to cry. She cries because the mean streak that has caused me to say the same attacking thing over and over has not changed, even though I've been a Christian for years. Maybe I try to perk her up by offering to take her out to eat after church. After all, I have to get her to stop crying before we reach church—because how would it look for a "good Christian man" to walk into church with a wife whose mascara is dripping down her chin?

Suppose my wife even takes the "spiritual high road" and says in her heart, "Father, forgive him, he has no idea how much he hurt me." She wipes her tears, and we go into church. Even though we're together *physically*, there is a huge emotional chasm between us. She cannot rest fully when she's with me because she cannot trust that I will not pulverize her spirit again.

But suppose I come to my senses, and I see my destructive tendency. Suppose I say, "God has shown me how wrong I was to say those hurtful remarks. I was wrong, unloving, disrespectful, and insensitive to you. Can you find it in your heart to forgive me?"

If she believes I am sincere—and if I live in a way that demonstrates I meant what I said—then the relationship is restored, maybe better than ever.

In Richard's case it became clear that he was not truly repentant. He was only sorry for the consequences of his sin: He was sorry he ruined a chance at love. He was sorry Sandy didn't want to see him anymore. But he wasn't sorry that he had persisted in order to get his own way, that he had pressured Sandy to do something she really did not want to do. Or that he had violated God's moral standards concerning sex.

I put it to him this way: "What if you were presented with an identical situation again? Suppose you were on the beach again with Sandy and everything was 'right.' Would you have sex with her?" He had to admit that, *yes*, he probably would. His answer revealed a wide gap in his character. Even though he knew it would be wrong, he probably would do it again. He had no true remorse—only a bit of guilt and sadness that his blunder had cost *him* something wonderful. So he couldn't forgive himself because he knew deep inside he really was no different.

Genuine repentance is not superficial. It involves a deep level of sincerity. It requires asking God to show you the depths of your heart, where the emptiness or need lies that you are choosing to try to fill with sinful actions.

Do you find yourself relating to Richard's style of repentance? Is it tempting to just apologize—but refuse to do the inner work necessary to get fully to the bottom of the problem? It is not enough to ask forgiveness for being domineering if the true underlying problem is an ego that always wants to be in control out of fear of losing someone. Repentance means that you stop using someone and damaging that person as you seek to fulfill your own self-centered needs and desires.

As we begin the process of change, we must not only root out the motives of our wrongful behavior, we must also be willing to make proper amends for our actions. This will create the opportunity to restore a relationship, if possible, with the other party. Genuine repentance, then, opens the door to confession, restoration, and a clear conscience. Ultimately it provides healing for feelings of spiritual burnout. This process can be greatly assisted by a spiritual counselor or pastor who can help us see our blind spots and hold us accountable.

Guilt-Motivation

One of the primary sources of burnout, as we have discussed, is guilt. The church and the Christian community, unfortunately, can sometimes help to intensify this guilt by using it as a "motivational tool."

Suppose the pastor wants to start a program of personal evangelism. He feels the members of his church are not "sharing their faith." He sets up a program of evangelistic training and announces it to the congregation. He may say it blatantly or by innuendo—but the message is clear: "If you are spiritual you'll get behind the evangelism training class. If you don't, you are unspiritual and there is reason to question the sincerity of your faith." Can you feel the pressure?

Maybe it's a new building program to add space for more Sunday school classrooms. Suppose you question the program or the timing. Or you think it is too ambitious, given the size of the church. Too often the response of church leadership can be, "Don't you have enough faith to believe God can do this? Don't you trust your elders to know the mind of God? Isn't the spiritual thing to do to follow your elders' leadership?"

Don't get me wrong. I am not against evangelistic training or new church buildings. What I am opposed to is the use of *guilt-motivation* that weighs people down and causes spiritual burnout. *Grace* is a much-preferred motivation. Maybe we can see it better in contrast.

Take Bible reading. Guilt says, "You have to read your Bible or you're unspiritual." Grace says, "You get to read your Bible for spiritual growth." Guilt says, "Tithe or your business will fail." Grace says, "God loves a cheerful giver." Guilt focuses on outward performance and appearance. Grace focuses on inner realities and getting the heart into a right relationship with God.

Sadly, people often burn out on the church because they sense they cannot honestly admit their faults, or they think they're unable to live up to the ideal standard set before them. In actuality, they sense they cannot admit their *humanity*. They don't get the support they need because they are not allowed to be honest about their flaws, hurts, and failings. Perhaps they are not allowed to disagree with the leadership without being labeled a rebel.

We need to experience a climate in which we can rest in the acceptance and grace of God. We need to move into a spiritually honest and supportive atmosphere where we assist one another in warding off the destructive voices of condemnation. This is the recipe for renewal in Christ and a perfect antidote for burnout.

For Thought and Discussion

1. What does a guilty conscience feel like to you? Is it possible to *be* guilty and not *feel* guilty?
2. Can you identify "rationalizations" you have used to justify doing what you know is wrong?
3. What effects does guilt have on you? What part does repentance play in healing the effects of guilt?
4. Is there something for which you need to forgive yourself? What steps do you need to take?
5. Have you ever felt that a church leader was using guilt to manipulate your behavior?

Setting the Anchors

David Hawkins

I have always appreciated the philosophy of Adventures Northwest, a company that takes teenagers out into the wilderness to teach them survival skills. After three weeks in the wilderness, the kids have a new appreciation for the outdoors and a renewed sense of self-confidence to overcome difficulties. It's part of the strategy to take the kids to the edge of their abilities and beyond. The staff tries not to tell the kids what to do, but lets them discover by trial and error the best way to perform survival tasks.

One of their survival skills is setting up their shelters at night. Every year there are a couple of kids who are careless in setting up their tents. Rather than drive the tent pegs deep into the ground, they simply find a big rock and set it on the rope line that holds the main pole of their tent. The staff could tell the kids what will happen when the night winds blow up the canyon—but they let the kids find out for themselves. It is not long after the lights are out that the breeze picks up. And soon the careless campers' tents blow over in the wind. It is always a ruckus and quite funny as they try to scramble out of a collapsed tent. However, it teaches them a good lesson. The next night they take the time to drive their tent pegs into firm soil so that it will withstand the night breezes.

There is a lesson to be learned from this for us as men. Many of us haven't given much thought to the "setup" of our lives. We do things in a "makeshift" manner. We don't *really* pay attention to life's most important things, like

- building strong friendships;
- making growth steps in our career;
- growing in both the knowledge and practice of our faith;
- building up and guiding our children;
- learning how to love our wives—*and* how to tell them what it is we need without being overbearing or demanding.

Consequently, when disappointment and burnout strike, our flimsy life collapses. Only we aren't adolescents anymore on a summer survival camp. It is our life.

The good news is we can set some substantial "anchors" that will hold us and enable us to weather future storms. Sometimes it's only by experiencing major burnout that we find out what's truly important. Then we can rediscover core values that can withstand any storm.

Here are eight anchors that are necessary to keep your life stabilized and moving in a healthy pattern of growth and maturity. If you construct your life on these anchors—or commitments—you will avoid future burnouts and crippling disappointments. We recommend that you make commitments to *authenticity, time, community, faith, forgiveness, gratitude, self-care, and solitude.* These commitments come out of scriptural principles that have to do with both outer actions and inner attitudes. Let's consider how they apply to the stabilizing and restoration of a man's life.

Authenticity

Whatever circumstances have gotten us to the place of disappointment and burnout, we now have the chance to dis-

cover or become stronger in our core motivations or commitments. The truth about who we are and who we will become
must rise to the surface now.

Who *are* you? What are you committed to—*really*? Maybe
you've never really known.

One of the ways to determine the course that fits us best is
to really *know* who we are. For so much of our lives we have
been *told* who we are, what we enjoy, and what we are to be
doing with our lives. Or we have been driven by selfish desires
and impulsive actions. Now we need to listen carefully to how
we have been made and what direction God would suggest for
our lives. This process involves living in *authenticity*.

Do you know what your core values are? Have you taken
the time to honestly discover what drives you and why you
make the choices that you do? Do you know what your true
passions are, or your spiritual gifts? Is your life directed from
your areas of giftings? Theologians used to use the word
accidie to describe the sin of failing to do with one's life what
one knows one could do—which leads to boredom, depression, and despair. Many of us are ambling through life rather
blindly. How do we get to know who we really are—and what
our core values are?

Take the time to examine your most dominant emotions.
For instance, what makes you angry? The fact that you get angry is a clear indication that one of your core values is being
violated. Or do you find yourself isolated and feeling bored?
That can be an indicator that you value working in community. What do you fear? What's exciting? The answer to these
questions provides clues to your value system.

Jesus put it this way: "Where your treasure is, there your
heart will be also" (Matthew 6:21). Where do you invest your
time and energy? What do your daydreams and conversations
reveal about the goals and accomplishments you value the
most?

Many of us value one thing, yet do another. We say family
is most important, yet we spend the majority of our lives at

work or escaping into hobbies. We say we value our relationship with the Lord but fail to give Him even a small portion of our time. We say recreation and friendships are valuable to us, yet we fail to adequately care for these areas of our lives. Living authentically means taking an inventory and aligning our lives with our true values. There is a new kind of vitality that comes to our lives when we are living, working, and growing in what we deeply value. And a new strength that helps us withstand setbacks.

So, what are your core values? Are they worth living for? Are they a source of struggle for you? How can you live in alignment with truly worthy core values?

Stewart and Randy were neighbors. They lived side by side in the cul-de-sac. Both had good jobs; both had young families; both attended the same church.

Stewart had recently become interested in how large fortunes were made by prominent families in America. He read the biography of John D. Rockefeller. Inspired by this multimillionaire's life, Stewart began collecting works of art. He bought Standard Oil stock. He even hired a maid to help around the house.

Randy, on the other hand, had read the biography of George Müller, a true giant of the faith from England. He was impressed by the simple lifestyle and sincere faith that Müller exhibited. When he looked at all the unused toys and bicycles cluttering his garage, Randy felt bad. If George Müller had two clocks, he'd sell one and use the money for the needs of the orphanage he had opened. "I only need one clock to tell time," he said.

It so happened that both Randy and Stewart took family vacations during the second week of June. When they returned home, both were shocked to discover that their homes had been burglarized. Apparently some experienced thieves had backed in a semi-truck and stripped both houses clean! They took *everything*—the microwaves out of the wall, even the carpet off the floor. Fortunately both men had insurance that covered most of the loss.

Stewart went into deep depression—he felt violated. His treasure was gone; his world wasn't safe anymore. He was heartsick over the loss of his works of art. Those were not replaceable. He made an appointment with the pastor because he was so depressed he wasn't able to function.

Randy, on the other hand, said, "After some minor refurnishing, I still have enough money left that I can give to missions. Besides, I wanted to live a more frugal life anyway. The robbery just made it easier." Randy made an appointment with the pastor to find out about missions. He wanted to give his money to a worthy cause.

You can see how these two men have different core values.

Time

Some of the men we've been talking about live to work rather than work to live. They have been "storing up treasures on earth"—as Jesus put it—as if this is where they are going to be setting up their tent for a long time. They have failed to consider the true meaning of time. They have not yet learned to live with eternity's values in mind.

Consider with me the difference between action and contemplation. When we live purely active lives, our time is spent moving about the world and acting upon it. When we learn the art of observation, some time is spent in observing the world and letting its lessons and realities impact us.

During my busy work weeks I am very aware of chronological time—*chronos*. I have appointments to keep and a schedule that seems to rule my life.

However, when I am off for the day and out on the lake on my Sunfisher, I am more aware of *kairos*—time made spacious and gracious by the presence and larger perspectives of God. Out on the lake I am aware of the beautiful hillsides that reflect light in different ways. I'm aware of the timeless rhythms of water and wind. Times of relaxation and reflection like this help to restore a larger perspective to me: Regardless of tensions, stresses, disappointments, and losses, there is peace and stability in some measure in the simple patterns of God's creation. When Jesus wanted to teach us how to stop worrying about the wild fluctuations of our bank accounts, He told us to *consider* the flowers of the field and birds of the air (Matthew 6).

When things don't happen according to our schedule or the way we want them to, we need to renew our commitment to God's schedule and His way of working on the longer timeline of our lives.

I am also aware of *kairos* time when I am enjoying a time of contemplative prayer. While still a newcomer at contemplation, I remain quiet instead of reading God a laundry list of what I want or telling Him what I think He should do. I am lost in the presence of God, and chronological time has little meaning. I am only interested in being still and letting the awareness of God, His might, His plans, and His goodness act upon me.

One of the anchors we need to reset is the anchor of time. We need to see time in different dimensions—not just as something we must wrestle into a schedule for our control. While we can still "make the most of our time" because it is passing, we also need to open ourselves to the restorative perspectives of eternity—the realm in which God lives and moves and unfolds His plans for us and the world we live in.

Community

Much of what we have come to understand about disappointment and burnout has to do with the issue of isolation. We were not created to spend our lives in isolation, and when we find ourselves outside of community, we become vulnerable to all sorts of problems. *Community provides for us a sense of healthy challenge and protection.* Isolation leaves us without support—and without the perspectives of others to balance us out.

Community involves many different aspects. Included in our concept of community is a sense of cohesive family life, a groundedness in church life, seeing our work in a larger context, and an involvement in the larger community. Without this stability most men feel lost with a sense of loneliness and personal futility. While we may pride ourselves in being individuals, the truth is that we need one another. Without the challenge and support of community we are vulnerable to poor choices and an increased tendency to imbalanced living.

Another important aspect of community has to do with the issue of worship. When we spend our time on Sunday in the presence of other believers, we remember our identity as people of God. When you and I are enmeshed in feelings of disappointment and burnout, it's tempting to let this part of our spiritual life die, yet dropping out of church only further exacerbates the problem. We need to worship God—and we need to spend time with other Christian men praying, searching for God's will, and learning how to live honestly in His presence.

From Scripture, we see the role of community in the early church. Acts 2:42–47 says the men and women of the early church

- were committed to a relationship of fellowship;
- wanted lives guided by the Word of God;
- shared their belongings with one another;
- gathered for the breaking of bread and meeting the needs of the poor;
- wanted to spend time in prayer for one another;
- owned possessions in common so they could have more resources to share with people in need.

The early church saw the value of community, and we can anchor ourselves in a commitment to shared visions, goals, and group support.

Faith

Most of us have spent years managing our lives by ourselves. Some of us know where this self-involvement has gotten us. One of the stakes we need to drive deeper into the soil is that of *faith*. By that we mean *putting our whole lives into the hands of God.*

Life will repeatedly tempt us to rely upon our own resources. But we must remind ourselves that there is One who is capable of managing our lives in a way impossible for us.

Just as our core values are revealed by tension or disappointment, our real faith can be revealed at such times, too. Consider Jairus. In Mark 5, we read the story about Jairus's daughter who was dying. "Please come and put your hands on her so that she will be healed and live," Jairus pleaded. So Jesus went with him. On the way, however, a woman who had been bleeding for twelve years—and who had suffered under the care of many doctors—came up behind Jesus and touched His cloak. Immediately, we read, her bleeding stopped, and "she was freed from her suffering." When Jesus saw who had touched Him, He said, "Daughter, your faith has healed you."

Soon after, some men came from the home of Jairus and told Jesus not to bother to come because the little girl was dead. Again Jesus said, "Don't be afraid; just believe." He went on and raised the little girl from the dead.

These stories have some important lessons about life for us, especially as we are recovering from disappointment and burnout. Jesus Christ is concerned about our well-being. We know men—maybe we have been men—who have tried to make it on their own, utilizing all of their resources. But the Great Physician, the Helper, our Lord, will come to our aid if we call on Him with confidence and self-abandonment.

Have you found yourself at the end of your natural resources? Can you—with self-abandonment—reach out to Jesus and trust that He knows exactly what you need? Are you willing to diligently seek Him out and ask Him what it is you need? Faith in Christ is one of the deepest, strongest anchors that will give you stability and renew your soul when life disappoints your expectations.

Forgiveness

Anger, resentment, bitterness, and the impulse to have vengeance are like consuming fires in a man's soul. Negative feelings can become a deadly downward spiral.

Forgiveness is one of the anchors that offers us inner freedom. The commitment of grace to forgive opens up the wells of grace. Forgiveness allows us to go and get on with life instead of hanging on to old grievances.

Josh was a middle-aged man who had developed a close friendship with Bob in high school. They had finished school together, spent two years in the army together, and then went to college together.

As Josh and Bob grew older and developed their careers, their friendship was even more entrenched. Their wives had to accommodate their friendship, as it was one of the most important things in their lives.

Unfortunately a crisis hit. After years of friendship, their relationship was stretched beyond capacity. Bob became temporarily involved with Josh's wife during an opportunity of closeness. Feeling immediate, crushing guilt, Bob confessed it to Josh.

Josh was crushed. The two families were driven apart over the situation. And after years of a close and rewarding friendship between the couples, the division left terrible pain.

Just as destructive as the affair was Josh's inability to move on with his life as months passed. Try as he might, he could not adjust to the devastating betrayal of his wife and best friend. He could not stop obsessing about what had happened, and his heart was filled with rage, hurt, and bitterness.

While no one can fault Josh for his pain, he also chose to imprison himself in unforgiveness. Attempts by his wife and by Bob to make amends fell on deaf ears. Josh was stuck and had lost any joy or inner freedom.

Pain and betrayal always drive us into self-centeredness and a defensive stance. But we cannot live there. Bitterness or hostility are unhealthy emotions to anchor our lives upon. True, it takes time to move through a trauma, and efforts to forgive prematurely can backfire on us.

Eventually Josh was able to process the pain of betrayal in a way that was satisfactory to him. Josh had to wrestle with his pain and accept that other people could fail him greatly. He was finally able to see the suffering his wife and friend were going through and to accept that he too is a sinner and prone to failure and in need of forgiveness.

Once you and I learn how to make an attitude of forgiveness one of our life commitments, a new health comes to our soul.

Gratitude

Mike always complained about his job. He worked for a large manufacturing plant. The place was too hot in the summer and too cold in the winter. The rotating shift was impossible. His boss was "a jerk," and the guys he worked with were "worthless." He'd been bad-mouthing his job for fifteen years—but never took any steps to make peace with his job or find a new one. Complaining just became a bad habit that toxified his whole attitude, his conversations, and his family, too.

Because of an energy crisis, electricity to the plant was reduced. The company began laying off workers, and Mike lost his job. The economy in the region was in a slump, and he couldn't find work. His unemployment insurance wasn't enough to meet all their bills, and Mike had to take his kids out of the private Christian school. He also had to sell his Jeep and some of his best hunting rifles just to keep the lights on and food on the table.

Mike didn't realize how important his job was until he lost

it. Complaints came easy when the checks came in. When the checks were gone the job didn't look so bad. Fortunately for Mike, within the year the plant expanded operations again and he got his old job back.

You don't hear Mike complaining about his job—or much else—anymore. As a matter of fact, he openly expresses how nice it is to have regular work. Sometimes it takes hitting a major pothole to show us what's really important, that is, *the ability to appreciate what we already have.* God is sometimes like the staff of Adventures Northwest in that when He sees we have put up a flimsy tent, He allows a stiff wind to blow it down so we can establish stronger anchors next time—with a change in our behavior and with revised values.

One of the anchors for life is *gratitude.* It is no accident that the New Testament pulses with the beat of thanksgiving, regardless of how trying the circumstances. Paul says, "Give thanks in all circumstances" (1 Thessalonians 5:18). When we make an attitude of gratefulness to God a priority even in the most difficult of times, we open ourselves to the renewing work of His Spirit in our lives.

Our natural tendency is to be grateful for only "the good things" and to complain about the tough parts of our lives. This artificial division of life leaves us unable to be shaped, strengthened, or changed by the "bad" things, or to see how God works in our lives with grace and power to make us the men He wants us to be.

Why not take time today to look around and see what's happening in your world? What could the hard things teach you? What blessings have you lost sight of? Can you begin to acknowledge it all as a gift from God?

Self-Care

Self-care is seldom thought of as a primary anchor in restoring or rebalancing our lives.

We would like to review several areas that need our attention.

An attitude of hopefulness. Having an attitude of hopefulness will open our lives to possibilities for growth. Conversely, attitudes of hopelessness and powerlessness create a mindset where we expect the worst to happen. A negative or cynical mindset leads to depressing fatigue, doubt—even physical illnesses.

Do you need an "attitude check"?

Care for your body. It has been clearly demonstrated that proper exercise, sleep, nutrition, and rest all contribute to your mental and emotional well-being. If you are like most men, a sedentary lifestyle causes weight to escalate and moods to de-escalate. Most guys reach an age when they can no longer eat anything in sight or ignore the nutritional value of the foods they ingest.

If we want to be as free as possible from disease and live optimally, we must pay attention to keeping our bodies healthy and fit.

Living in balance. Perhaps the most difficult thing for any man is balance. We need times of challenge, times of play, times of pursuing creativity, with consistent breaks and vacations from work. We need to balance spiritual growth with making progress in our outer lives.

Think about it: How balanced are you?

Caring for relationships. It has been well established that happiness is tied directly to the quality of our relationships. Given that, it makes sense for us to give extra care to our marriages and other important relationships. Isolation or tension in relationships leaves us vulnerable to the effects of life's many stresses.

Spiritual well-being. It is worth saying again. Our spiritual lives play a central role in how we will fare emotionally. Our recovery from stress, disappointment, and burnout can be greatly enhanced by establishing a deeper relationship with God and others in a community of faith.

How would you rate your life on the above qualities? Do you feel as though you have been caring for yourself, or is this something that needs more attention in your life? Can you see some places to begin?

Solitude

Our final anchor is a commitment to seeking re-creative solitude.

Solitude provides us a means of stepping back and gaining perspective. It gives us time to sort things out. To think. To realize how the events of life have impacted us. A chance to plan what our response will be—and to identify confusion and questions we still need help answering. Solitude can mean *only* escape—but solitude *with* reflection is re-creative.

When we are facing new challenges in our lives that require increased decision-making, time alone can be invaluable. In silence and freedom from distraction, our creative energies and openness to God can help us to find new solutions and solve problems. In solitude there is a re-creation that cannot happen in any other way. We need to learn that it is all right to want to spend some time alone, and that it is both therapeutic and soul-restoring.

Consider including into your life a daily time of prayer, journaling, and contemplation. Find out what works for you. Do what works, and don't do what doesn't work.

But *do* determine what you need to do to build time and activities into your life—activities that will balance re-creative rest, with careful consideration of the way your life is going.

Why not take some time right now to consider what commitments you need to make to gain a balanced, healthy life?

For Thought and Discussion

1. In what ways have you not lived an *authentic* life? Where have you not lived in accordance with strong, healthy core

values? Have some of your values placed position, power, or possessions before *people*? Even before your own physical, emotional, or spiritual health?

2. Do you have a grateful heart? How can you cultivate *more* gratitude?

3. Reviewing the list of self-care guidelines, in which areas are you strong? Where do you need improvement?

4. How comfortable are you with solitude? How would you describe your prayer life?

How Do You Get Your Way?

Ross Tunnell

In an earlier chapter we looked at some of the ways that life smacks into every one of us—at the disasters, setbacks, and heartbreaks of life on this planet. It was a big revelation to me that I was not going to live a "charmed" life, and that God was not going to build an invisible barrier around my house so that the sun always shone on me while rain fell on the "unspiritual" guy next door. Learning how to cope with tough realities is a living skill every mature man needs to learn. Without a strong spirit focused on inner strengths, the gritty circumstances of life will defeat you.

David and I have also introduced you to some of a man's hidden enemies from within—the drives that are out of balance, the ambitions based on superficial values. In this chapter I want to help you look at another big source of disappointment and burnout—that is, the twisted ways some of us go about trying to get what we want from other people. I am talking about *manipulation*.

Some of us have learned a kind of relationship subterfuge. We know what we *want*—but we carry a constant fear that we're not going to get it. And so we come up with *other ways* to angle for what we want. Basically, there are two kinds of manipulators—guys who take the *direct assault approach*, and guys who take the *indirect approach*.

The guys who manipulate to get what they want by direct assault use anger and loudness—and they may even use their physical size and muscle power to intimidate other people into doing what they want. If you are using physical strength in a brutish way with anyone—especially your wife and children—get professional help immediately. If this is a problem for you, you have gone beyond manipulation and are using abuse to force people to do what you want. There is no justification whatsoever for physical abuse. Seek the help of your pastor *and* a professional counselor. Even if you are a few steps short of using hands or fists, and you are in the habit of using high-powered blasts of attacking words to instill fear, intimidation, and compliance, get help now for your anger. Long-term emotional abuse is extremely harmful to women and children. This includes using shame and guilt, name-calling, and threats to pummel another person's mind, emotions, and spirit.

Sad to say, even good Christian and churchgoing men are plagued by anger that erupts volcanically in harmful, aggressive behavior. With professional help and personal accountability you can change and find healthy, constructive ways to deal with anger before it wreaks devastation. Don't wait if this is true for you. *Get help today.*

Men who use an *indirect approach* to get what they want are also afraid to speak up and ask for what they need. They merely use less obvious means. They use hints, self-pity, nagging, pouting—or the veiled threat that they'll have to go find someone else to help them out, a *replacement* for the person who "should" be filling the role. Men like this also withhold affection, approval, involvement in others' lives—in short, they take the passive-aggressive route and withdraw in a sad attempt to play on someone's sense of duty, obligation, or personal guilt as a motivating force.

Both *aggression* and *passive-aggression* are huge factors that contribute to disappointment and burnout in a man's life. And yet we use these unhealthy "techniques" with our wives and kids, our bosses, our siblings, and our friends. Rather than learning the healthy adult skills of relationship negotiation—which include wins, losses, trade-offs, and draw—we hold on to the childish notion that we have to find ways to win what we want all the time. But that is not the truth: life, in reality, includes give and take, wins and losses, delaying gratification, even sacrifice for the sake of another or for a larger purpose.

Men, when stuck in a win/lose mentality, are like little boys who have not glimpsed the mature truth about life itself. We burn out ourselves and others with our demands. And we live in constant disappointment with jobs, people, and ourselves.

Maybe you're thinking, *I'm not a manipulator. . . . I'll skip to the next chapter.* HOLD IT. You could be missing one of the most important parts of this book if you exclude yourself now. Read what follows and honestly evaluate what "techniques" you may be using to get what you want in unhealthy, relationship-draining ways.

Meet a Manipulator

I am a world-class manipulator. I've done it all my life. That is my qualification for writing this chapter. It wasn't until approaching the middle years of my life that I realized how manipulation has weakened me and my relationships.

Manipulation means using influence or pressure to cause another person to do something they don't want to do. If the person were free to choose, they wouldn't do it, but because of pressure, they cave in and do the will of another. Manipulation is what we do to *control* another person's action.

Manipulators win battles—but they lose the "war." You may get what you want, but you won't want what you get. What you get is a person or situation that only yielded to pressure, deceit, guilt—not because you had the healthy living skills to actually *win* in the situation. The manipulator may get what he wants outwardly, but he knows in his heart that he had to deceive to get it. He *loses* because he can never enjoy his gain with a clear conscience.

I am appalled at how quickly I can resort to manipulation to get what I want if I'm not on guard. Manipulation is a result of self-centeredness: I manipulate when I forget to keep the needs of others in view.

As I illustrate various manipulative techniques, you might see yourself in them. If so, take time to consider the serious and often devastating results of your actions. The first step to correcting a problem is always recognizing that there *is* one.

For instance, I have a need for physical affection. If my wife says she isn't "in the mood," I have to "get her in the mood." If I ignore her need for space and her promises of attention later, I will resort to *techniques* in order to get what I want now. The following are three techniques that I am ashamed to admit I have used, trying to get my wife "in the mood."

1. I take out the garbage. Yes, that's right, I take out the garbage. Why? Because I am *bartering*. I'm saying, look what I've done *for you*—now you have to do what I want as payment. She sees me tippy-toeing to the garage carrying the garbage sack with a smirk on my face. She doesn't have to stop and wonder, *What does he want?* She knows, because a "coded" message has been sent: "I've done you a favor, now . . ."

Other acts of kindness men use with an ulterior motive may be a gift of flowers, candy, an evening out with dinner and a movie, jewelry, vacations—or just giving in to his wife's emotional requests . . . with a "bill" attached.

Of course, it's right to take out the garbage, give gifts, or please my wife. But when I am maneuvering to get my needs met, the ulterior motive taints the act. *Why* am I doing these things?—that's the clue as to whether or not I am being manipulative. Am I giving because I genuinely care and want to love and be a supportive husband? Whose needs am I really focusing on?

2. Another tactic I've used is to mope around the house with a long face, pouting and slamming doors. Sooner or later (hopefully sooner) she gets tired of my whining and gives in. In fact, I get what I want—but the emotional needs and relational needs of our marriage suffer because of the selfish motivation behind it. The pursuit of self-gratification puts a strain on any relationship.

3. A third tactic I have used is to make up an emotionally wrenching story to illustrate what I want.

Let's say that I want my wife to take some initiative regarding physical affection. In my wife's case, because of her emotional makeup, she will say, "I respond best when you take the initiative. And besides—I feel it's not feminine to be the initiator."

Anticipating that response, I decide in advance to wring her emotions a bit. So I resort to the story of when I was a little boy and used to ride my tricycle up and down the sidewalk. One day I fell off my tricycle and skinned my knee. My mom heard my cry and ran out of the house, scooped me up, and took me into the house. She washed my wound, put on some medicine—and then she rocked me to sleep. Boy, did I feel loved!

After telling the story I could say, "Even though I'm grown, I sometimes feel like that little boy with a skinned knee. I want you to come along and make it all better."

In that case, I'm hoping my wife will feel sorry for me and take the initiative. But knowing that someone helped you because of pity is pretty demeaning and only detracts from a man's inner need to be strong.

And that's always the problem with manipulation. It will almost always hand you a counterfeit, and not the thing you really need. And it ruins the giver's respect for you.

Another Bag of Tricks—Blame

The oldest—and probably the first—manipulation tech-
nique ever used was *blame*. Our first parents used this choice
weapon on each other, and even on God. When Adam was
caught in red-handed disobedience, he first focused on Eve,
then turned to blame God. "It was the woman that you gave
to me"—yes, it was the woman who made him do it, but ultimately it was God who is responsible. After all, God brought
the woman to the man. (And who did Eve blame? The snake!)

There is one thing about this kind of reasoning that we all
agree on—*it is not our fault*. The other guy is to blame. The
boy blames the girl, and the girl blames the boy. The parent
blames the child, and the child blames the parent. The student
blames the teacher, and the teacher blames the student. Or we
have the audacity to blame God.

But the Word of God shines the light of truth on us: "For
from within, out of men's hearts, come evil thoughts, sexual
immorality, theft, murder, adultery, greed, malice, deceit,
lewdness, envy, slander, arrogance and folly" (Mark 7:21–22).
In reality, it is nobody's fault but mine.

Let's take a close look at this.

When I say, "You make me mad," I am trying to blame you
for my anger. More truthful is the fact that you can't make me
mad. I am only using a given situation as an opportunity to
express anger I already have on the inside. *Circumstances do
not determine my spiritual state; they only reveal it.* The
neighbor's dog that dug up our flower garden can't make me
mad if I don't choose to get angry. The dog is giving me the
opportunity to express anger that comes from within. If I come
running out of the house, swearing at the dog, it is not the
dog's fault. "For out of the overflow of the heart the mouth
speaks" (Matthew 12:34). I have a heart problem. My actions
tell the truth—it's me, not you. Blame only postpones facing
the truth about yourself.

My point in all this is to try to persuade you not to blame
others for what is clearly your fault. It is not your wife's fault;

it is not your boss's fault; it is not your pastor's fault. It is *your* fault. Pointing the blame to someone else will keep you in a spiritual quagmire for a long time. Accepting responsibility for your actions is the right thing to do and the only way to stop playing the blame game.

"Mr. Volcano"

Recently in our adult class at church the teacher explained two essential ingredients for marital satisfaction. One is a high level of mutual affirmation. The second is *a good working system of conflict-resolution.*

After class I told my wife I thought we were doing pretty well in both categories. She turned to me with a shocked look and said, "Do you *know* what our conflict-resolution system is?"

"Yeah—we talk things through," I answered.

"No. When we have a conflict, you get angry and I withdraw."

Now, that made me mad!

Recently a local church offered a free class on "anger management" for men. The church has a large, competent counseling staff that prepared the material. Only two men called to inquire about the class, and they very warily wanted to know what the curriculum was and who the instructors were. But neither signed up. During the same time, several dozen wives called to see if there was some way they could get their husbands to attend.

What does that tell you?

If your wife is sensitive and easily hurt or intimidated or not a "confronter," then it will be tempting to use your anger to get your way. Does anger define the limits of your relationship? Do you serve notice that you are not to be criticized or you'll blow up? Do you get angry if your wife makes a request—like asking you to spend more time with the kids? Are you open to a discussion about your place as spiritual leader in the home—or when your wife brings it up, do you get mad?

Maybe you're the kind of guy who still thinks that anger is working *for* you. *It is not.* Getting what you want by turning into "Mr. Volcano" destroys love, trust, and peace.

"Or Else . . ."

Billy was from the "big sky" country of Montana. He was a regular "Marlboro Man." Riding around in his pickup truck, chewing tobacco, and wearing a ten-gallon hat, he looked the part. His swagger and attitude completed the picture. His wife, Susan, was initially attracted to him because of his "rough" manliness—but that grew old real fast.

When Susan made a mistake, Billy would mock her. "How could God make someone so beautiful to be so stupid?" She would always answer, "God made me beautiful so you'd marry me, and he made me stupid so I'd marry you." The truth was that Susan *did* feel stupid for having married Billy. The only thing she felt grateful to Billy for were their three children. But she wanted more out of life.

Billy was happy with his construction job. Susan always had dinner ready, and afterward he'd plant himself in front of the TV until bedtime. That was his typical day, and he loved it. Occasionally he'd show up at church—"just to keep Susan off my back."

It was probably a foolish (and manipulative) way to get Billy's attention. But Susan admitted to him one night that their marriage was a disappointment—and that she'd been feeling an attraction toward "a nice guy" at church.

Billy went haywire. He began ranting and raving about what he was going to do. Ultimately he threatened to hit her where it hurt most—he threatened to take their three children and move away where she'd never see them again.

Ultimatums and blackmail never allow real issues to come to light. Threats do not rebuild and heal. A relationship held together by threats is no real relationship at all—it's two people held together by emotional handcuffs.

Are you a guy who resorts to threats and "emotional leveraging"? Decide right now to hang it up. If necessary, get help.

Approval

If you are married to a woman who craves approval, you may have learned how to withhold approval to get what you want. Whether it's your wife, a parent, or a child, some people will do almost anything to get approval. So all we have to do is *withhold* approval until they do what we want. Perfect. Some men go so far as to use "love" as the litmus paper: "If you loved me, you would . . ."—fill in the blank with your wants. If you loved me, you wouldn't ask me to go to your mother's house. If you loved me, you would cook the food I like. If you loved me, you would let me use our savings to buy . . . On and on it goes.

This scam comes to a close in a couple of ways. Let's say you're using it on your wife. Someday she'll wise up and turn the tables on you. If *you* loved *me*, you would take me out to dinner instead of making me slave over this hot stove!

Or your wife may grow up emotionally and realize she doesn't have to have your approval to feel good about herself. She may become her own person and decide for herself what she wants to do or not do.

When we make people jump through our hoops to "measure up," prove their worth, or demonstrate their love, we have turned them into performing animals for our own ends. Wrong. Wrong. Wrong.

If this has been your game, it's time to stop.

———

Face it, men. Manipulation may work *temporarily*—but it is spiritually bankrupt because it lacks the essential ingredients of love and respect. Love focuses on the best interest of the one loved—and it respects her enough to allow her to make her choices freely and without pressure. Manipulation fails us, too—because in the end we painfully learn that our techniques have gotten us a substitute for the genuine article we were really after.

Manipulation wears us out from within—because it cannot buy relationships, respect, and honor before God.

Though it takes every bit of courage and integrity you can muster, learn to be a straightforward, reasoned man. Let the "little boy" in you—who wants to manipulate—grow up.

For Thought and Discussion

1. Have you ever been manipulated? Describe your feelings.
2. What are some needs you have a hard time talking about or asking for in a straightforward manner?
3. What can you do to get your needs met instead of using manipulation?
4. What attitude do you really have toward the person—man or woman—who you know you can manipulate to get what you want?

Maintaining Your Inner Balance

David Hawkins

Many of us can identify with the same struggles as the men in this book. We have experienced fatigue from unrealistic expectations or the belief that we could be all things to all people. We've burned out trying to chase dreams or trying to impress someone. We're worn down by our own manipulations, by not being true to our spiritual values, or by poor self-care habits and lives out of balance.

In our disappointment or weariness we've tried to fill our interior void with *something*. All of us have been searching in various ways for the same thing—peace, well-being, and a sense of release from the inner tensions that drive us. In this final chapter we want to offer you some guidelines for finding peace and freedom from being driven. This is not to say that is simple. It is not. But hopefully you have begun to gain some insights as to where you are most likely to fall prey to forces that will wear you down—whether from stresses from without or weak areas from within where you need to grow and be strengthened.

When it really comes down to it, if you are like us, you want peace and inner strength more than anything else. All of

the other toys and accolades that you can collect are nice—but
they do not replace a sense of well-being and purpose. In the
final analysis, most of us would give anything to have a sense
of real excitement about life again. It is more than possible.

We want to leave you with a simple and powerful tool that
you can use every time you find yourself becoming overwhelmed by disappointing, wearying circumstances. "The
Serenity Prayer" is a powerful guide for millions of men who
have recognized the forces from without and within that can
overwhelm their inner stability and drive them to unhealthy
ways of dealing with life. You do not have to be overwhelmed
by failed dreams, drives to succeed, or a sense that others *must*
give you what you want.

"God, grant me . . ."

It is not clear who actually wrote "The Serenity Prayer,"
and it may date back to the fifth century. The theologian Rein-
hold Neibuhr is usually credited with writing it—but there are
records that indicate he gave credit for it to Friedrich Oetinger,
an eighteenth-century theologian. In 1947, Niebuhr read it in
an obituary notice in the New York *Tribune*. He apparently
liked it so much that he shared it with Bill W. (founder of Alcoholics Anonymous), who adopted it for that program. No
matter who wrote the prayer, it has provided many with inspiration, direction, and steps to renewal.

Even if you think you don't like "written" prayers, consider the simple truths that are so powerfully conveyed in
these few words:

> God, grant me the serenity
> to accept the things I cannot change,
> the courage to change the things I can,
> and the wisdom to know the difference;
> Living one day at a time;
> Accepting hardship as a pathway to peace;
> Taking, as Jesus did, this sinful world as it is,
> not as I would have it:

Trusting that you will make all things right
if I surrender to your will;
that I may be reasonably happy in this life
and supremely happy with you forever in the next.

—Amen.

This prayer focuses us on the one source of true peace, ful-fillment, and freedom. Is it time for you to take the focus off yourself and turn it to God? For most of us our problems orig-inate when we believe we can manage our own lives. We se-cretly reject the Lord of life and try to find life in some object or purpose. Those objects, visions, and goals may not be sinful in and of themselves—but when they become gods to us, they push out the only unfailing source of inner well-being and life: God himself.

Receiving from God is something that is difficult for most men. We may try the daily devotional plans. But they fail to help us learn how to rest in the presence of God. We need to begin to look closely at our fear of being in the presence of God. Are we afraid we'll lose ourselves or be asked to do some-thing we're not prepared to do? Or that we'll be asked to give up something we don't want to give up?

Many men find different forms of prayer helpful as they search for new ways to "be" in the presence of God. For my world to quit rotating around me I have to sit with "Him."

When we learn to be still in His presence, we experience His profound love for us in fresh ways. Is it time for you to approach the Scriptures in new ways? Can you set aside any guilt you carry and consider what the apostle Paul meant when he said that God has "rescued us from the dominion of darkness and brought us into the kingdom of the Son he loves, in whom we have redemption, the forgiveness of sins"? (See Colossians 1:13–14).

Serenity

What is *serenity*? For many the first thought that comes to mind is some trancelike state. Or perhaps you think of some guru sitting in the lotus position without a care in the world.

Serenity is really the opposite of burnout. It is the opposite of being in the middle of a spinning world, feeling the crash of chaotic circumstances. It is a calm assurance, being directed from within, unshaken by external events.

What would it be like to possess a mind that is not racing, cluttered with worries of today and tomorrow? Consider that there is available to you a way to slow down and to slow your mind down—so that you are not always one step ahead of yourself. Would that sense of tranquillity be worth anything to you? Would you like to fall asleep at night and wake up the next morning feeling deeply, truly rested? That is possible for you.

Jerry was a man who had been overinvolved in nearly every aspect of his life. He couldn't say no to any request made of him. He had very good intentions and got a lift out of helping people in need. He did not have to go far to find them. His own extended family always had problems and often looked to him for their answers. Jerry was a "rescuer"—to the dismay of his wife and children, who often got the leftovers from him.

During a men's retreat at church, Jerry was introduced to the concept of a "quiet time" with God. It was a real stretch for him at first to sit quietly for even the fifteen-minute exercise at the retreat. But encouraged by the peacefulness of the weekend experience, he took home some tools he learned and has been practicing daily prayer for over two years now.

There have been many benefits for Jerry—but the most practical has been his new ability to stay more focused, letting God do more of the work in people's lives, rather than responding impulsively to his own inner need to "rescue." As a result, others in his family are learning to help themselves. Jerry is not feeling so burned-out, and he has a more balanced approach to life. His wife and kids appreciate the energy he now has to give to them.

Acceptance

The prayer encourages us to "*accept the things I cannot change.*" What a simple and obvious concept. Who would want to struggle against things they could not change?

We all do at times. Most of us do not stop long enough to find out what we can and cannot change. So we often find ourselves railing against things we have little chance of impacting. The fight becomes draining . . . and the result is burnout. Burnout always results from taking on a challenge that we have little chance of changing. A futile effort—even if done with the best of motives—will drain and disappoint us.

Jerry's inner stability developed when he accepted the fact that he could not change others. For instance, he could not change his brother and sister-in-law's troubled marriage. They would often call on him when they were in a serious dispute that often involved physical confrontation. But try as he might, he could never persuade them to attend counseling, church, or other programs that might help them resolve their marital struggles. His frustration mounted as they continued in their destructive patterns, while calling on him to bail them out when things got too rough. Jerry reluctantly took the counsel of his pastor—which was to pray for them and to help them find professional assistance when they were ready for it.

When Jerry *accepted* the fact that he had no power or expertise to change things, the tension drained out of his life, and peace returned.

Acceptance. Most of us men need more than one lesson. We need to learn not to take on everything as a personal battle. We do not need to be heroes. We do not need to be so competitive and win at everything we do. We can learn to let some things go. More important, we can learn which pursuits are worthy of our best efforts and which ones we should pass up.

As you read this, consider what issues get you riled up. Maybe you've tried to change something and your efforts have been futile. Maybe you've been told to "back off," "slow down," "let it go!"

The opposite of acceptance is *control*. Maybe you're sick of hearing that word. Your spouse, children, and others have told you that you need to quit being so controlling. "But," you plead, "I'm just trying to make things go the way they should go."

Yes, in an ideal world your boss would appreciate all of your efforts and give you due recognition. In an ideal world your spouse would not defend your children against your authority. People would act the way you want them to act, and you would not feel the need to chastise, scold, nag, or manipulate. But then an *ideal* world would not be under your control, would it?

Do yourself a big favor and learn which things are beyond your control. Learn which issues are really yours, and which ones are best left to others who need to learn to care for themselves.

Courage

For some men the bigger issue is the need for *courage*. "The Serenity Prayer" directs us to have the courage necessary "to change the things that can be changed."

Now, we are not talking about fruitless, wasted energy—but energy keenly directed toward something we can influence.

Too many of us, unfortunately, not only expend energy in the wrong direction, we refuse to expend our energy in the right direction. Some of us are frightened of taking on any challenge or confrontation. Family and personal problems overtake us, and still our voices are silent. We each live with situations where we have stepped back, hoping that someone in "leadership" will take the reins. We refuse to step out on the front lines.

And so we need to call on God to grant us the courage to take action when action is needed. In our families, where there is distress and a lack of leadership. In our place of work, where perversion and dishonesty are commonplace. In our church, where a new breed of men is needed for direction. Courage to face personal habits that cause us guilt and shame and drain us.

You may be wondering how to *begin* to change.

The way to begin is to start small. Make a list of the areas of your life needing change. Take the time to sort out the list of those things you can change and those you cannot change. For some this can be overwhelming, so do not even imagine that you should try to change your whole life all at once. That's a sure formula for failure and discouragement.

On the other hand, you can isolate one major situation that needs your attention. Perhaps you will start by talking over your struggles with a friend so that you are not so isolated. You may need to say no to overly demanding people in your life. You may want to take a college course to prepare you for a job change needed to be made in the future. There are many ways to begin to change, and there is no one right way.

One small step of courage leads to larger steps. But *you* must begin.

Wisdom

"The Serenity Prayer" encourages us to have the wisdom to know the difference between what we can affect and what we cannot control.

This begins, for the Christian man, when he develops the wisdom to know what is worthy of his pursuit. What will bring eternal value—rather than just fleeting pleasure?

How do you get life wisdom? Someone has aptly stated that wisdom is the result of experience—and experience includes risking making mistakes and learning.

Solomon, in the book of Ecclesiastes, shares his troubled path to wisdom. He pursued worldly accomplishments, sensuality, learning, food and wine—and in the end wisdom told him that nothing under the sun can fill the empty places in a man's life but learning serenity in God's presence. Solomon seems to have let one compulsion after another rocket him through life.

After burning himself out, Solomon learned.

Wisdom is gained from experience mixed with learning how to listen to God in the inner places of our heart. The means and the goal of wisdom is to develop a soul that knows how to quietly trust God to lead us step by step through the areas of change that are right for us. In our own strength we are not going to know what is right. But as a result of meditating on His Word, being still before God, and seeking the counsel of godly men, we can have assurance of His guidance.

Living One Day at a Time

Serenity and inner fortitude come to those who learn to live one day at a time. Besides making common sense, Scripture assures us that this wisdom is true. Jesus said,

> Therefore I tell you, do not worry about your life, what you will eat or drink; or about your body, what you will wear. Is not life more important than food, and the body more important than clothes? Look at the birds of the air; they do not sow or reap or store away in barns, and yet your heavenly Father feeds them. Are you not much more valuable than they? Who of you by worrying can add a single hour to his life? . . . Therefore do not worry about tomorrow, for tomorrow will worry about itself. Each day has enough trouble of its own. (Matthew 6:25–27, 34)

"Living one day at a time" is one of those simple truths we can all wrap our arms around. It makes sense.

Ask God for the wisdom that helps you focus on today's issues today. Let go of the past.

Accepting Hardship As a Pathway to Peace

In life, hardship is going to come our way. Try as we might to escape problems, we would be much better served to learn how to deal head on with problems.

So often men want to give up on their marriages, believing they would be better off in another relationship. But not long after they're in a new relationship, they find that their problems have attached themselves to their backside. There is no escape from problems, and if we only rail against them or blame them on someone else, we don't learn to embrace them as part of our lot and learn how to deal with them.

The notion that hardship is a pathway to peace is, quite frankly, a notion most of us rebel against. We dislike the idea that it will take hardship to teach us some lessons we would much rather learn our own way. But as we have said earlier, it often takes a *breakdown* for there to be a *breakthrough*. Would that it were not so—*but that's the way it is!*

Begin to consider how your struggles can change you in a positive way. Learn to let your problems work on you. When you do so, you allow your character to be changed—and that requires the slow, gradual process of struggle.

Trust

Finally we would like to exclaim with the writer of "The Serenity Prayer" that God will make all things right if we surrender to His perfect will.

This is not some pie-in-the-sky notion or a spiritual placebo. Trust is a *verb*. Trust is something we strongly encourage you to practice. Practice trusting that if you listen for His will every day and set your issues before Him in prayer, He will lead you on the path of change and new direction.

If you are like most men, *letting go of outcomes* is the hardest part. We have a chosen destiny in mind and a timetable for getting there. That will not work with God. He will make all things right in His own time—*if we surrender!*

Trust means that we let go of our own agendas and listen for how the Lord wants to direct our lives. In the past our self-will has run riot, and now we are ready to turn our lives over to Him. It is time for our egos to take a backseat to the One who can adequately manage our lives.

Renewal

Men—we live in a time like no other, where most of us are feeling rushed, pressured, imposed upon, and fatigued. We are drained and need to be recharged from the depths of our being. We have let down our boundaries and taken on more than we can possibly handle. There is more noise in our lives than silence. There is more clutter and chaos than serenity. Like Jesus himself, we each need to pull ourselves away for a time of reflection and reconsideration of our values, priorities, and mission. We cannot hold to our present course of drivenness and struggle without feeling spent, used up, and worth little to ourselves and others.

We invite you to consider a profound redirection of your life. A chance to follow your true passions and gifts and feel refreshed and alive.

Blessings.

Do it—*now!*

For Thought and Discussion

1. In what areas have you expended energy that was fruitless? What signs of burnout did you receive?
2. What does "letting go" mean to you? Where in your life do you need to "let go"?
3. What are the areas in your life where you need courage to change? What is stopping you from moving forward? What is one thing you can do today to start the change process?
4. So far on your journey, what has been the major hardship in your life? What has the hardship taught you?
5. Consider the idea of trust. How easy or hard is it for you to trust God? In what area of your life would you like His help?
6. Meditate on Proverbs 3:5–6: "Trust in the Lord with all

your heart and lean not on your own understanding; in all your ways acknowledge him, and he will make your paths straight." What do you think the Lord would have you trust Him for *today*?